# KINGDOM DISCIPLESHIP

## PART 1

## BEING A DISCIPLE

L. Douglas Dorman, Ph.D.

LEADER SPACE
ALIGNING HEARTS WITH GOD'S PERSPECTIVE

# TABLE OF CONTENTS

Dedicated to Joan Dorman

# Acknowledgements

J OURNEYS BEGIN WITH a first step. Joan and I began our missional journey on 19 October, 1986 when Joan Watson Dorman and I said, "I do", and the rest is . . . children. Thirteen months after "I do", on 30 November 1987, John Michael arrived; he was soon followed by Corrie Lois, Laurel Elisabeth, Nathan Douglas, Ian Shepherd, Charis Joy, and Charlotte Gray 14 years later on 17 November 2001. Joan and I wanted to do our part declaring the gospel of the kingdom, so we figured seven continents—seven kids. Grandkids started coming in 2018 to our delight. The multiplication effect began with "I do."

From 1986—2003, our family of nine planted churches or served in staff positions in a variety of churches in South Carolina, North Carolina, and Georgia. In 2004, we launched Your Next Step as a discipleship ministry, and in 2013 Joan and I joined staff with Global Training Network to encourage, equip, and empower leaders, pastors, churches, and families around the world.

God used family, friends, authors, leaders, and pivotal thinkers to shape my understanding and development of *Kingdom Discipleship*. I came into a personal relationship with Jesus Christ in April 1972[1]. Five years later, I experienced an empowering of the Holy Spirit on 2 April, 1977. When I said "I do" to Jesus, my personal discipleship journey began. God brought disciplers, mentors, coaches, and teaching alongside me from the start. He also used printed materials, audio recordings, conferences, and ideas to shape my understanding of discipleship.

As a teenager, I wanted to share everything I was learning with my friends. I started a Bible study in my home when I was 14 using

---

[1] Sunday, 2 April 1972 was Easter—I was nine years old; on Sunday, 23 April, I received baptism.

1

Derek Prince's *Foundation Series,* and Frank and Ida Mae Hammond's *Pigs in the Parlor,* a book on deliverance. My eighth grade English teacher encouraged me to reach my friends, so when I learned something new, I believed I had a responsibility to pass it on to others.

In college and seminary, Robert Coleman's writings impacted my understanding of discipleship yet further by systematizing Jesus' approach. A few years later when I entered vocational ministry, Robert Clinton, Ralph Neighbour, Jr., Bill Beckham, Neil Anderson, Jim Egli, Henry Blackaby, and Linus Morris significantly shaped my understanding and approach to disciple making.[2]

Many friends who helped me flesh out *Kingdom Discipleship* deserve special mention: Tim Holt, Don Bulla, Jeff Dunn, Roy King, Sarah Southern, Kevin Childs, Albert Nathaniel,[3] Tim Fall, Dusty Reynolds, Dane Moore and the entire Sycamore Church in Savannah, Georgia served as much needed guides along the path. A huge thank you to Lottie Dorman for designing the cover and creating the icons throughout *Kingdom Discipleship.* I am also grateful for David Lones and his editorial expertise. Places where you find errors are the clearest evidence of my work not David's. The list falls short of being complete, but it does make a dent in it.

*Kingdom Discipleship* roots grow deep in the soil of family, friends, and lifelong learning.[4] Knowledge, concepts, and ideas fall short of developing mature disciples; discipleship consists of more than information. Knowledge, outside of the context of loving relationships, puffs up and proves fruitless. I am thankful for the symbiotic relationship between information about God and conversations with those who know him. The first, knowledge about God, may be found in books; but the second, friendships with those who know him, flourishes around cups of coffee and tea.

THANK YOU to my family and friends for helping me move from

---

[2] In 1997, I met Linus and our friendship began. We've traveled in Europe, Africa, and South America together. God's used Linus to deepen and broaden my understanding of discipleship, leadership, mentoring, church planting, and multiplication of movements more than anyone else. I am most grateful for the gift of friendship.

[3] Sarah Southern, Kevin Childs and Albert Nathaniel left the scene for heaven earlier than I hoped; I miss them greatly. Their premature departure from the earth scene increases my longing for the "not yet" of the kingdom. I look forward to our reunion.

[4] My family accuses me viewing my books "as family"—guilty as charged.

being a disciple, to making disciples, to multiplying disciples, leaders, churches, and movements—you laid the foundation for *Kingdom Discipleship*. My earnest prayer is for many to grow more deeply in love with Father, Son, and Spirit as they apply what they glean from the Kingdom Discipleship Series. Let's begin, say "I do" to discipleship.

Take Your Next Step,

L. Douglas Dorman

# PRELUDE

T HE BIBLE UNFOLDS the story of God's Kingdom, his rule and reign. The triune God—Father, Son, and Spirit, speaks the world into existence, "Let there be light." God creates the world as an exciting place meant for relationships, fruitfulness, exploration, and adventure; he uses the words "very good" to describe his handiwork. God places Adam and Eve, the first humans, in a garden and invites them to rule and reign with him.

God tells Adam and Eve they may eat from any tree in the garden except one—"the tree of the knowledge of good and evil"; however, they reject God's plan and seek to live life independent of the God who made them and loves them. Adam and Eve's indifference to God's goodness results in their disobedience and introduces death into the world.

God immediately responds by reaching out to rescue and restore Adam and Eve, and continuing to reach out to their descendants. Genesis 1-3 tells the story of creation, the fall, and God's plan to rescue and restore, and Genesis 4—Revelation 22 tells the rest of the story. Ultimately, God the Father sends his Son, Jesus Christ, to set things back to right. God the Father, and God the Son send God the Spirit to dwell within followers of Jesus and reignites the original plan for the world given to Adam and Eve, to be fruitful, multiply, and fill the earth—Habakkuk echoes the plan in his own words, "For the earth to be filled with the knowledge of the glory of the LORD as the waters cover the sea," Habakkuk 2:14.

Jesus Christ the Son, the perfect God/man, reveals how life in the kingdom operates by healing the sick, casting out demons, and teaching his disciples, his followers, how to do the same. Jesus models for us how to live life according to his divine design. Jesus lives a perfect sinless life, dies a shameful death, is buried in a borrowed tomb, and reverses the curse of death by rising from the dead.

*Kingdom Discipleship* invites you to be part of God's plan of drawing the world to the Father by proclaiming Jesus as the Christ through the power of the Holy Spirit. You will learn how to yield your life to God, pray for the sick and see them healed, cast out demons, and teach others about God's amazing love. We invite you to embrace your calling, to live the life you yearn for, the life God created you to live—life in the kingdom.

# INTRODUCTION

*Kingdom Discipleship* consists of three parts:

## Part 1—Being a Disciple

> Jesus said to him, "I am the way, and the truth, and the life. No one comes to the Father except through me." **John 14:6 ESV**

Jesus' closest disciple, John, gives us a great template for what it means to be a disciple; in 1 John 2:12-14, he clearly outlines a path toward spiritual growth and development. John uses relational language to describe the spiritual process of moving from being a child in the faith, to growing as a youth, to reaching maturity as a parent—who helps others in their journey with Jesus.

> "So, if the Son sets you free, you will be free indeed." **John 8:36 ESV**

John says spiritual adolescents "overcome the evil one." God desires us to walk in freedom. John emphasizes spiritual teens know how to overcome the evil one and how to be strong in moral character. Week three provides a spiritual inventory revealing, and giving tools to address, deep hurts, stubborn habits, and emotional hang-ups in our lives. When our hurts, habits and hang-ups remain unaddressed, they hinder our growth and development. Untangling ourselves from hinderances empowers us to fulfill our life calling.

## Part 2—Making Disciples

Jesus said,"Go make disciples of all nations." **Matthew 28:19 ESV**

The book of Romans provides a missional map, a practical guide, moving followers of Jesus from being disciples to making disciples. In the first half of Romans Paul tells how Jesus Christ rescues and restores those who **come** to him; in the second half of Romans he focuses on Jesus' followers' call to **go** out in Jesus' name to rescue and restore others.

## Part 3—Multiplying Disciples, Leaders, Churches, and Movements

Jesus said, "You will be my witnesses in Jerusalem, and in all Judea and Samaria, and to the end of the earth" **Acts 1:8 (ESV)**

*God desires for you to be fruitful and multiply!* The book of Acts provides a model for moving beyond being a disciple and making disciples to multiplying disciples, leaders, churches, and movements. The book of Acts models how the early disciples used Mobile Apostolic Training Teams (MATTs) to push the kingdom beyond local expressions to global explosions. Understanding your gifting and how you fit on teams, empowers you to live the book of Acts once again. At times, you may feel your growth seems slow, but hang in there, ***progress in the process equals success!***

## Kingdom Discipleship will help you understand . . .

- How to be a disciple
- How to share your faith with others
- How to study and apply the Bible individually and in community
- How to overcome hurts, habits, and hang-ups so you can help others
- How to engage meaningfully in personal prayer, and how to pray for the sick
- How to discern God's will

- How to discover and function in your gifting as a team player
- How to make disciples relationally
- How to multiply disciples, leaders, churches, and movements using MATTs

**Things you will need for this study**

- A Bible
- A Journal
- A Set of colored pencils including yellow, green, blue, red, and brown.

*Kingdom Discipleship* works best in community. Who do you know who can join you on the journey? Invite a friend to join you one-on-one in your home or at your favorite coffee shop, or form a small group and meet together once a week to discuss how you are applying the material in your life.

Here are some questions you can use in your weekly meetings to facilitate reflection, conversation, and action.

- What did you learn about God this week?
- What did you learn about yourself?
- What is Your Next Step?
- Who do you need to share this information with?

# WEEK 1—DAY 1
# THE APPLE

**Matthew 28:16-20** NASB "But the eleven disciples proceeded to Galilee, to the mountain which Jesus had designated to them. And when they saw Him, they worshiped *Him*; but some were doubtful. And Jesus came up and spoke to them, saying, 'All authority in heaven and on earth has been given to Me. Go, therefore, and make disciples of all the nations, baptizing them in the name of the Father and the Son and the Holy Spirit, teaching them to follow all that I commanded you; and behold, I am with you always, to the end of the age.'"

## AN APPLE

Hold an apple in your right hand, if you do not have an apple—picture one in your mind.

**"What do you see?" Write down as many details as you can think of—aim for 10 observations.**

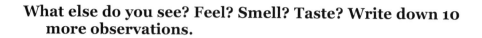

**What else do you see? Feel? Smell? Taste? Write down 10 more observations.**

**Look again. What potential does the apple hold? Write down what comes to mind.**

Some may say, "An apple." Others might add, "A red apple", or "a green apple." Someone might say, "An apple pie", or "A tree;" another might expand the possibilities, "An orchard." An orchard, hmm, or "orchards." An apple holds seeds with the potential to reproduce orchards. *Kingdom Discipleship* resembles an apple filled with seeds.

God planted seeds in your heart when you surrendered to Jesus. Father and Son implanted the Spirit in you. The triune God programed you with dreams, visions, gifts, talents, skills, and desires—seeds. God designed you to bear kingdom fruit—God wants his kingdom in you to grow into a life of fruitfulness.

As you grow, your life will influence many others who will also bear fruit producing more apples, trees, and spiritual orchards until Jesus Christ returns in the fullness of his kingdom. Dream big. If you let the truths presented here take root in your life you will be amazed at how God includes you in his great adventure.

God desires to multiply disciples, multiply leaders, multiply churches, and multiply movements around the world. As you learn and apply the practices found here, your life will become part of the mathematical equation.

# THE KEY WORD IS **MULTIPLY.**

**Discipleship takes a lifetime . . . but the journey begins with your next step.**

Take your next step in prayer by *pausing just a moment and asking God to include you in his global adventure. Prayer is simply talking with God the same way you'd talk to a friend. In your own words, ask God to involve you in his activity. Then watch to see what happens next.*
When we become followers of Jesus, disciples, he accepts us as we are, but he does not leave us as he found us. He places his Spirit within us to help us grow and mature. He desires to move us from being disciples to include us in making disciples. God is all about, "Turning Disciples into Disciple Makers," but I'm getting ahead of myself.

**Kingdom Discipleship aims to fulfill three purposes.**

- **Encourage you** to implement a **relational model** of discipleship able to reach your entire family and friend group
- **Equip you** with **sticky tools**—we use symbols, illustrations, and stories—to help the content stick
- **Empower you to lead others through** *Kingdom Discipleship* **locally and globally**—by embracing both/and thinking—you will influence your family, friends, and complete strangers **both** locally **and** globally

## Relational

When we look at the life of Jesus, we immediately notice he begins with 12 guys. He calls these guys "disciples", and he engages with them relationally. They go to weddings, to the beach, fishing, and to funerals (he messes up more than one good funeral by raising people from the dead). Jesus calls brothers to follow him—Peter and Andrew—James and John. Nathaniel shares the same zip code as Peter, Andrew, James, and John. Jesus calls these five guys, and six others, his friends.[5] Jesus clearly values relational ministry.

*Kingdom Discipleship* seeks to follow the relational approach of Jesus by emphasizing one-on-one connection with a friend, or with a small group of friends, to go through the material together. Using *Kingdom Discipleship* as a solo study truncates its, and your, potential. You are wired for relational community.

## Sticky

In the next few pages, you will encounter illustrations designed to help you learn. Since Jesus uses symbols, images, metaphors, similes, and stories to communicate ideas, we do too—the apple at the beginning of today's lesson serves as metaphor #1.

*Kingdom Discipleship* utilizes colors and diagrams as "learning hooks" to help you grasp key concepts and ideas. Over the next eight weeks you will learn how to reproduce these key ideas through story, illustration, or my favorite, on a napkin at Starbucks. Once you learn the key illustrations, get your pen handy and start presenting your drawings to others. Get in the habit of immediately reproducing what you learn. The quicker you present the images for a family member or friend the faster you grasp the concepts yourself. You might call our approach "napkin theology".

## Local and Global

Jesus desires for the world to know him; the world includes your family, friends, neighbors, and the whole earth. Check out God's global promise in the two verses below.

---

[5] The twelfth guy, Judas, was not present for the friendship conversation.

"For the earth will be filled with the knowledge of the glory of the LORD, as the waters cover the sea." **Habakkuk 2:14 NASB**

"But you will receive power when the Holy Spirit has come upon you; and you shall be My witnesses **both** in Jerusalem, and in all Judea and Samaria, **and** even to the remotest part of the earth." **Acts 1:8 NASB**

Notice the progression of Acts 1:8. The verse begins where the original disciples live and then radiates outwardly to include the ends of the earth. The movement clearly radiates from local engagement to global influence. Jesus expects both local and global impacts.

Now you know the vision of *Kingdom Discipleship*. Tomorrow, we will examine four key sections of scripture looking at Jesus' requirements for discipleship. Pause right now and ask God to give you a heart to grow and obey him.

KINGDOM DISCIPLESHIP

# JOURNAL TIME

Use your journal (or the space below) to write down:

What did you learn about God today?

What did you learn about yourself?

What is Your Next Step?

Who do you need to share this information with?

# WEEK 1—DAY 2
# A DISCIPLE IS . . .

**Matthew 4:19** (ESV) *"And he said to them, "Follow me, and I will make you fishers of men."*

**Matthew 28:18-20** (ESV) *And Jesus came up and spoke to them, saying, "All authority has been given to Me in heaven and on earth. Go therefore and make disciples of all the nations, baptizing them in the name of the Father and the Son and the Holy Spirit, teaching them to observe all that I commanded you; and lo, I am with you always, even to the end of the age."*

JESUS SPEAKS HIS final command clearly to his disciples; he says as you are going, *"make disciples"*. The process includes going, baptizing, and teaching. But what is a disciple? How does Jesus define discipleship?

According to Jesus, a disciple is a lover, learner, loser, and leader.

**A Disciple is:**

1. A disciple is a lover who has a desire to love others

"By this all people will know that you are my disciples, if you have love for one another." **John 13:35 ESV**

In your journal (or below), sketch a picture of what comes to mind when you think of someone who loves others well.

2. A disciple is a learner who has a hunger for the Word of God

> "So Jesus said to the Jews who had believed him, 'If you abide in my word, you are truly my disciples, and you will know the truth, and the truth will set you free.'" **John 8:31-32 ESV**

In your journal (or below), draw a picture of what abiding in the word of God means to you.

3. A disciple is a loser who has a willingness to leave lesser things[6]

> "If anyone comes to me and does not hate his own father and mother and wife and children and brothers and sisters, yes, and even his own life, he cannot be my disciple." **Luke 14:26 ESV**

---

[6] No, Jesus does not see you as a "Loser", rather he calls you to let go, loose, anything hindering your walk with him.

"So therefore, any one of you who does not renounce all that he has cannot be my disciple." **Luke 14:33 ESV**

What do you think Jesus meant by these words? Was he being literal? Was he using hyperbole? In your journal (or below), write or draw a picture of what comes to your mind regarding this difficult passage. What do you need to let go of?

**4.** A disciple is a **leader** who has a heart to lead others to Jesus

"By this my Father is glorified, that you bear much fruit and so prove to be my disciples." John 15:8 ESV

Who do you have a heart for? Jot down in your journal the names of those you desire to see come to know Jesus.

## JOURNAL TIME

Of the four (Lover, Learner, Loser, Leader), does one cause you more trouble than the others? Take a few moments and pray through each of the scriptures mentioned today. Talk with Father about your relationship with him and about your struggle with the requirements of discipleship. Be honest about your struggles. Father will not be surprised.

## REMINDER

*(If you have not already done so, you will need to purchase a set of colored pencils for tomorrow. Be sure your pencil set includes yellow, green, blue, red, and brown.)*

# WEEK 1—DAY 3
## THE COLOR CODE

THE FOLLOWING FIVE COLORS and symbols will help you to identify major themes and patterns throughout the Bible.

Yellow

Green

Blue

Red

Brown

Your Next Step is a discipleship ministry my wife, Joan, and I started in 2004. Your Next Step grew out of our years of working as church planters. Your Next Step's Mission is:

- **Bring them in**
- **Build them up**
- **Send them out**
- **Publicly, and House to House**

For someone to become a follower of Jesus, a disciple, the Holy Spirit must draw them to the Father through the Son—Jesus Christ. When I became a follower of Jesus Christ, I was nine years old. My burning passion became, "tell others." God uses the process of telling others as his primary way of bringing people into his kingdom.

## BRING THEM IN

Bring to the Father (Bring people into the kingdom)

**Yellow Sun**
The symbol of "the sun" and the color "yellow" represent bringing others into the light.

*"For the Son of Man came to seek and to save the lost."* **Luke 19:10 (ESV)**

*Jesus said to him, "I am the way, and the truth, and the life. No one comes to the Father except through me.* **John 14:6 (ESV)**

**Take your colored pencils, find Luke 19:10 and John 14:6 in your Bible.** Once you locate the two verses highlight both verses using your yellow pencil. These two verses epitomize God bringing others into the light of his love. After underlining or highlighting the verses in yellow, draw the symbol of the sun under or beside each verse as a reminder to yourself of God's desire **to bring others into his kingdom.**

When you share your story of coming into a relationship with Jesus Christ with others, God will use your experience to bring other people into the light of his love. The Bible frequently uses the metaphor of "walking with God" to describe our relationship with him. God uniquely designed you and your story so others can join you in walking in the light. Who do you know who is currently walking in darkness? Who needs to hear your story?

## BUILD THEM UP

Build others up in the Son (Build them up, or grow them up in the Kingdom)

**Green Tree**

*For we are God's fellow workers. You are God's field, God's building.* **1 Corinthians 3:9 (ESV)**

I grew up in a resort city, Myrtle Beach, South Carolina. During my childhood, I remember new homes and new hotels constantly popping up—like mushrooms—new buildings everywhere; my father owned a couple of those properties. However, dad came to city life late in life. When he was 51, he left farming for resort life. Paul, who wrote the book of Corinthians—quoted above—lived during a time when many people made their living through what they grew, but Paul also lived during a time when cities like Corinth were expanding rapidly. Paul mixes his metaphors in the verse above by using a rural agricultural example and a city example—God's field, God's building to describe the process of disciple making. We too use both ideas here, build them up—and then we show the tree as our image for growth—"God's field, God's building".

*Kingdom Discipleship* borrows from Paul's language and uses the concepts of building and growing interchangeably. God desires for you to grow, to spread out, to build, to multiply.

> *And what you have heard from me in the presence of many witnesses entrust to faithful men who will be able to teach others also.* **2 Timothy 2:2 (ESV)**

**Look up the 1 Corinthians 3:9 and 2 Timothy 2:2 in your Bible.** Highlight the two verses in green. Then draw the symbol of the tree under or beside each verse in your Bible.

## SEND THEM OUT

Send in the power of the Holy Spirit to proclaim the kingdom

**Blue Sky with a crown.**
The crown represents the kingdom. The cloud signifies our stepping outside into the world to declare the kingdom (Presumably under a blue sky).

> *And I heard the voice of the Lord saying, "Whom shall I send, and who will go for us?" Then I said, "Here I am! Send me."* **Isaiah 6:8 (ESV)**

*And Jesus came and said to them, "All authority in heaven and on earth has been given to me. Go therefore and make disciples of all nations, baptizing them in the name of the Father and of the Son and of the Holy Spirit, teaching them to observe all that I have commanded you. And behold, I am with you always, to the end of the age."* **Matthew 28:18-20 (ESV)**

**Look up Isaiah 6:8 and Matthew 28:18-20 in your Bible and highlight these two passages in blue.** Then draw the symbol of the crown and the cloud under or beside each passage.

God gifts each of us to accomplish his mission in and through us. He sends us out as gifted people to serve him and others. As we go out, may he give us blue skies. In America, we use a phrase, "The sky is the limit," meaning we seek to reach out as far as possible. God desires for us to reach out beyond our people group to multiply disciples, leaders and churches around the world.

# PUBLICLY

## Red Shepherd's Staff

*How I did not shrink from declaring to you anything that was profitable and teaching you in public and from house to house.* **Acts 20:20 (ESV)**

*I am the good shepherd. The good shepherd lays down his life for the sheep.* **John 10:11 (ESV)**

In 2008 I traveled to India for the first time. I met a man who quoted a couple of mission statements from large churches in the United States. How he memorized mission statements from churches thousands of miles away in a completely different culture baffled me. He asked me to tell him my mission statement. I said, "Bring them in, Build them up, Send them out, Publicly and House to House." He indicated he liked my statement. Then I asked him for his mission statement. I was unprepared for his answer. He said,

"Greater love has no one than this, Jesus died for me, and I will die for him." In 2017, he and his wife both died. Jesus said a good shepherd lays down his life for the sheep; they willing give their blood to spare the sheep. In honor of my friend who was a good shepherd, I use red, indicating a disciples willingness to spill their own blood for Jesus, as the color for the shepherd's staff.

Leadership takes place in both private and public settings. The Scripture uses the metaphor of a shepherd to refer to leaders. Moses, David, Jesus, Peter, and Paul each speak of leaders shepherding people. God calls us to be shepherds. He invites us to follow him by laying down our selfish dreams, agendas, desires, and very lives if necessary.

**Look up Acts 20:20 and John 10:11 in your Bible and highlight the verses in red,** then draw a shepherd's staff beside or below the verses in your bible.

# HOUSE TO HOUSE

**Brown Home**

*How I did not shrink from declaring to you anything that was profitable and teaching you in public and from house to house.* **Acts 20:20 (ESV)**

In traveling throughout North, Central, and South America, Europe, Africa, and Asia, I've seen homes of varying shapes and sizes. However, in each location, I noticed earthen homes and wooden structures with a natural brown color—therefore, we use brown to highlight "house to house." Journal a picture of your house.

Leadership starts at home. The home is where we begin making disciples. Joan and I married on 19 October 1986; we began using our home as a base for ministry from the beginning. **The home is a place where we cannot hide who we really are.** What would happen if your home became a center for ministry? Take a moment to journal any thoughts you have about using your home to minister to others.

"And they sang a new song, saying, 'Worthy are you to take the scroll and to open its seals, for you were slain, and by your blood you ransomed people for God from every tribe and language and people and nation, and you have made them a kingdom and priests to our God, and they shall reign on the earth.'" **Revelation 5:9-10 (ESV)**

The mission is to *Bring them in, Build them up, Send them out Publicly, and House to House.* The following chart gives examples of how to highlight your Bible according to these themes.

| BRING THEM IN | **EVANGELISM**<br><br>God is Loving and is in Charge | **God as Father**<br>Love, Grace, Reconciliation, Sin, Salvation, Sovereignty, Creator, Sacrifice, Atonement, Redemption, Baptism, Justification, Missions |
|---|---|---|
| BUILD THEM UP | **DISCIPLESHIP**<br><br>He has a Kingdom | **God as Son**<br>Revelation, The Word, Sanctification, Suffering, Growth, Money, Kingdom, Spiritual Warfare (Kingdoms in conflict), Personal Prayer, Health, Time Management, Sexuality, The Second Coming, Judgment |
| SEND THEM OUT | **MINISTRY**<br><br>His Kingdom Expands through His People (Both Israel and the Church) | **God the Holy Spirit,**<br>Gifting, Talents, Abilities, Israel as a People, the Church, Service, Helping the Poor, Caring for Our Planet |
| PUBLICLY | **WORSHIP (PRIVATE AND PUBLIC)**<br><br>God's People Need Leaders | **Leaders**<br>Public prayer, Worship, giving, leaders, leadership, Roles of Men and Women, Hearing God's Voice |
| HOUSE TO HOUSE | **FELLOWSHIP**<br><br>Leadership starts in the home | **Families**<br>Homes as Places for Ministry, Meals, Family, Husband and Wife, Children |

# LET'S PRACTICE HIGHLIGHTING USING THE COLOR CODE.

Turn in your Bible to Acts 2:42-47. Read through the passage and with your colored pencils highlight the themes you observe. Two examples are provided for you.

Example 1 -Verse 43 has blue because signs and wonders, miracles occur in this verse. When the apostles went out (Hint—under blue sky . . . memory technique—they proclaimed the kingdom). The apostles were sent out to proclaim and demonstrate the kingdom—they were sent out.

Example 2—Verse 47 points to people being brought into a right relationship with the Father—they were brought in.

## ACTS 2:42-47 NEW AMERICAN STANDARD BIBLE (NASB)

⁴² They were continually devoting themselves to the apostles' teaching and to fellowship, to the breaking of bread and to prayer.

⁴³ Everyone kept feeling a sense of awe; and many wonders and signs were taking place through the apostles.

⁴⁴ And all those who had believed were together and had all things in common;

⁴⁵ and they *began* selling their property and possessions and were sharing them with all, as anyone might have need.

⁴⁶ Day by day continuing with one mind in the temple, and breaking bread from house to house, they were taking their meals together with gladness and sincerity of heart,

⁴⁷ praising God and having favor with all the people. And the Lord was adding to their number day by day those who were being saved.

# JOURNAL TIME

Use your journal to write down:

Bring them in—Who brought you to Jesus Christ?

Build them up—How are you growing in your relationship with God?

Send them out—Who do you need to share Jesus with?

Publicly and House to House—Who needs you to shepherd them? When can you invite them over to your home?

# WEEK 1—DAY 4
# THE KEY PASSAGE

**The Key Passage**

*12 I am writing to you, little children, because your sins are forgiven for his name's sake. 13 I am writing to you, fathers, because you know him who is from the beginning. I am writing to you, young men, because you have overcome the evil one. I write to you, children, because you know the Father. 14 I write to you, fathers, because you know him who is from the beginning. I write to you, young men, because you are strong, and the word of God abides in you, and you have overcome the evil one.* **1 John 2:12-14**

**We observe a progression of maturity in 1 John 2:12-14**

When you read the entirety of 1 John, you clearly see John's emphasis on walking in the light and not walking in darkness.

## CHILDREN—HAVE BEEN BROUGHT INTO THE LIGHT

**What two characteristics do children have according to this passage?[7]**

## SPIRITUAL YOUTH—HAVE BEEN BUILT UP

**What three things characterize young men, spiritual adolescents?[8]**

## SPIRITUAL PARENTS—HAVE BEEN SENT OUT

**What one thing characterizes the fathers, spiritual parents, and what one thing is not mentioned but is implied?[9]**

---

[7] 1. Their sins are forgiven and 2. They know the Father.

[8] 1. Overcome the evil one, 2. They are strong, *moral character,* 3. They know the word of God

[9] 1. They know Him who is from the beginning (Jesus), longevity of relationship with God. 2. They reproduce (*Implied*).

The Bring Build Send model requires two social contexts:

1 **Public** or Publicly **and**
2 **Private** or Privately (House to House)

Large (Public) and small groups (House to House) provide the necessary environments for spiritual life to grow and develop. "Publicly" includes our large group gatherings of the church, but also our life out in the world—in the public sphere. "House to House" reminds us of the importance of using our homes as a place and base for relational ministry.

For the first couple hundred years after Jesus walked the earth the church met primarily in homes not buildings. The New Testament church met "Publicly and House to House;"—the public meetings included open spaces, i.e. the mountains, seaside, or fields, but homes provided the nucleus of the church.

Bill Beckham refers to churches meeting publicly and house to house as two-winged churches: A large group wing and a small group wing. Bill says a two-winged church will fly.[10]

***Children, Youth and Parents live out their faith in two environments—**Publicly and House to House*

AND

---

[10] I learned about the Two-Winged Church concept from Bill Beckham's Book, *The Second Reformation*.

## 3 Key Illustrations

- The Three Trees
- The 10 Periods (5 Pairs)
- The Stop, Look, and Listen Chart

Tomorrow, we will look at the first of our three key illustrations based on 1 John 2:12-14 -The Three Trees.

# Journal Time

Use your journal to write down:

What stands out to you in 1 John 2:12-14?

Where do you think you are in the journey?

Identify an area in your life causing you to feel stuck. Write about it. How does this passage and your need fit together?

# WEEK 1—DAY 5
## THE THREE TREES

R EAD 1 JOHN 2:12-14 and with your yellow pencil, highlight the sections of the passage mentioning spiritual children.

**Bring them in**

1 John 2:12-14

*Spiritual Children*
Sins forgiven
They know the Father

"For God so loved the world, that He gave His only begotten Son, that whoever believes in Him shall not perish, but have eternal life." John 3:16 NASB

Copy this verse, John 3:16, in your journal and memorize the verse.

I would like to tell you a story about three trees.

Well actually, it is a story about—

1—God
2—People and
3—Trees.

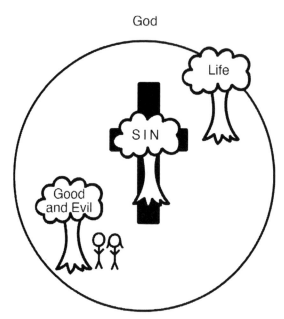

God creates the world and says of his creation, "It is good." Then God creates Adam and Eve and says of humanity "It is very good." The story is found in Genesis 1 and 2. God gives Adam and Eve tremendous freedom. They may eat from any tree in the garden except one—the tree of the knowledge of good and evil, but instead of obeying God, Adam and Eve chose to eat from the forbidden tree—see Genesis 3.

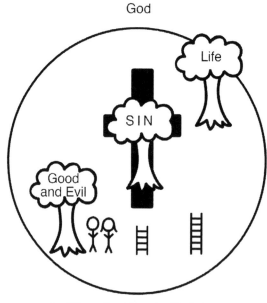

Indifferent   Moral   Religious

# 3 Types of People emerge as a result of Adam and Eve's decision

The first group shows indifference toward God.

## Indifferent People

Adam and Eve's indifference toward God causes a chain reaction of chaos, loneliness, sickness, confusion, and death; Genesis 4-11 outlines some of the destruction immediately following their disobedience. Perhaps you are, or someone you know is, indifferent toward God.

## Moral People

In Genesis 11, people build a tower toward heaven seeking to make a name for themselves (represented by the first ladder—The Moral person). Perhaps you are, or someone you know is, a good moral person. Moral people compare themselves to those who are worse than them. They may say, "I may tell a white lie, but I never steal;" or, "I may steal occasionally, but I've never killed anyone." Moral people grade on a curve.

## Religious People

The remainder of the book of Genesis, and the rest of the Old Testament, shows humanity's various religious attempts to please God or the gods (represented by the second—taller ladder. Religious people consider themselves as better than, above, moral people—thus the taller ladder). Perhaps you are, or someone you know is, a religious person. Religious people often measure life by dos and don'ts. As long as they do the right things and don't do bad things, they think they are okay.

**However, all three approaches fall short of God's standard of righteousness**; they are all rooted in self. The following three examples demonstrate how selfishness characterizes the indifferent, moral, and religious.

The **indifferent person** thinks God, if there is a God, is irrelevant; they don't need God. They can live a meaningful life without him. An indifferent person may say, "Do what feels good to you"—Anything goes.

The **good or moral person** feels they can live life by their own truth—as long as they don't hurt anyone else—they are good. After all they see truth as relative, "You have your truth, and I have mine." The moral person holds standards, but they set the standards.

The **religious person** meticulously follows the rules, and they hope their rule keeping will outweigh their rule breaking—Perhaps God grades on a curve. They hope their good deeds will be good enough.

The Bible calls all three of these approaches SIN; notice S-I-N is spelled with **"I"** in the middle.[11] You can't get more selfish than the life centered around "I". Even those who focus on serving others, measure their goodness by their actions—thus they still focus on themselves. Often their service reveals their attempts to gain merit with God or the gods.

In God's kindness, he provides a more fulfilling way to live. God's provision requires his Son to take our sin; so, we can experience his righteousness. Our merit with God is based on God's actions, not ours. The second tree represents Jesus' taking our sin upon himself when he died upon the tree.

"For God so loved the world, that He gave His only begotten Son, that whoever believes in Him shall not perish, but have eternal life." **John 3:16 NASB**

On the cross Jesus experiences separation from the Father (God's wrath); so we do not have to live apart from God. The good news is, Jesus does not stay dead on the cross. Jesus rose from the dead; so, we can receive his resurrected life. Jesus' life is available to you. Those who receive Jesus, receive his life; they are introduced

---

[11] I first heard Ralph Neighbour Jr. speak of sin having "I" in the middle.

to his kingdom—his rule and reign. Through Jesus, we are restored to right relationship with God the Father; we receive his righteousness.

God loves you and wants a relationship with you. Perhaps you feel separated from God. Maybe you've been indifferent toward God. Maybe you are trying to lead a moral life. Maybe you are religious. However, you've failed to reach God on your own. The Holy Spirit draws people to surrender their lives to Jesus in order to restore them to the Father. Perhaps he is drawing you right now. He wants you to be restored.

Those who surrender to Jesus, the Son, can eat from the third

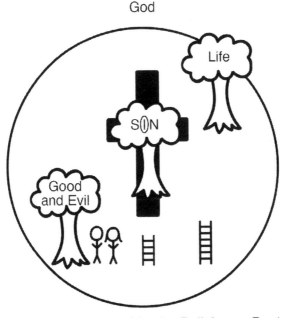

tree, **the tree of life**. The tree of life is introduced in the first chapter of the Bible and reintroduced in Revelation 22, the last chapter of the Bible. This is the good news.

The bad news is those who reject Jesus face eternal death, separation from God. God does not want you to be separate from him; he sent his Son to rescue and restore you. He invites you to eat from the tree of life. Access to life, represented here by the tree of life, is available to everyone who receives God's Son.

Here is a simple prayer to help you yield your life to God. By praying this prayer, you are affirming you want God's way—not your way.

***God, I give everything I know about me, the good, the bad and the ugly, to everything I know about you.***

And, what do you know about him? You know indifference, morality, and religion, fail to restore you to God. You know God in his love sent his Son for you. You know Jesus died and rose again to give life to you. You know yielding to him brings you into his forever family.

# JOURNAL TIME

Write down John 3:16 in your journal if you've not already done so.

Draw The Three Trees illustration.

Who will you share The Three Trees with? When?

# WEEK 2—DAY 1
# THE LISTENING ROOM

*Spiritual adolescents*
Overcome the evil one
They are strong
They know the Word

LOOK UP 1 JOHN 2:12-14 in your Bible. Notice the three characteristics John uses to identify spiritual youth. Take your green pencil and highlight the three characteristics of spiritual youth in the text.

When I met Joan, I wanted to talk to her every day; I still do. Talking includes listening; I had to learn this. Each afternoon we set aside a time to catch up on each other's day. Our daily conversations strengthen our marriage.

John says of spiritual youth, "they are strong." How do we grow strong spiritually? We acquire strength through a healthy prayer life, daily talks with God. Prayer includes listening—it's a two-way street. Prayer is not just **talking to God**; it includes **listening to his voice.** The following guidelines will help you develop a consistent and meaningful prayer life.

## MAKE AN APPOINTMENT WITH GOD

- Set a **time** to meet daily with God. Write it down.
- Set a **place** to meet. Jot down the location now.

## PART 1: BECOMING A DISCIPLE

Read through a passage of **Scripture** and ask God to speak to you. Why not read 1 John 2:12-14 again. What are three observations from the reading?

**Talk** to Father about your concerns, needs, and desires.

> Jesus said,
> 9 "Pray, then, in this way:
> 'Our Father who is in heaven, Hallowed be Your name.
> 10 'Your kingdom come. Your will be done, On earth as it is in heaven.
> 11.'Give us this day our daily bread.
> 12 'And forgive us our debts, as we also have forgiven our debtors.
> 13 'And do not lead us into temptation, but deliver us from evil. [For Yours is the kingdom and the power and the glory forever. Amen.'"] **Matthew 6:9-13 NASB**

Perhaps you have prayed this prayer before. It is often called The Lord's Prayer.

You can use The Lord's Prayer as an outline, or model for prayer as well. Rather than praying the prayer word for word, use the prayer as a template.

**Worship**, praise and thanksgiving

> "Our Father who is in heaven,
> Hallowed be Your name."

Take 5 or 10 minutes . . . Pick a song or two and sing to the Lord, give thanks for what he is doing in your life.

Write down the titles to the songs you choose.

## Ask for His rule and reign

"Your kingdom come."

Take 5 or 10 minutes . . . and ask for God's rule and reign in your life, for your family, in your job, etc.

Write down specific areas you are praying for . . .

## Ask for His will in your circumstances

"Your will be done, On earth as it is in heaven."

Take 5 or 10 minutes . . . and ask for God's will to be unveiled. Listen to see what he reveals.

What are your current circumstances? Put it in writing.

## Ask for daily needs to be met

"Give us this day our daily bread."

Take 5 or 10 minutes . . . and pour out your heart to your Father, let him know your needs. He is ready to listen.

List at least three of your needs.

**Ask forgiveness for thoughts, words or deeds not honoring to Him**

"And forgive us our debts, as we also have forgiven our debtors."

Take 5 or 10 minutes . . . tell Father about your failures. Ask his forgiveness.

What do you need to ask forgiveness for?

**Ask for protection from the evil one**

"And do not lead us into temptation but deliver us from evil."

Take 5 or 10 minutes . . . ask for the Fathers protection.

What areas do you need protection? Write them down.

## Close by declaring His kingdom

"For Yours is the kingdom and the power and the glory forever. Amen."

Take 5 or 10 minutes . . . and declare God's kingdom over your sphere of responsibilities.
What are at least three areas you are responsible for?

# Journal Time

In your journal, rewrite the Lord's prayer by personalizing it in your own words . . .

My rewrite . . .
"Good Father, you are the Head of our family, help us honor your name, seek your kingdom and do your will. Give us what we need to do these three things today. Forgive us when we fail to obey and let us extend forgiving grace to others. Don't let us fail—deliver us from the evil one. Yours is the kingdom, empower us to bring you glory."
Douglas Dorman

# WEEK 2—DAY 2
# HOW TO STUDY THE BIBLE

S O FAR, we have talked about how spiritual children know their sins are forgiven and how they know the father. Then we covered how spiritual adolescents find strength through prayer. Now we turn to another characteristic of spiritual youth. **They know the Word of God.**

**Build**

Turn again to 1 John 2:12-14. You may have noticed we did not yet cover "Overcome the evil one." We will take all of week three to deal with this important aspect of being a disciple.

### Children
Sins forgiven, They know the Father

### Spiritual adolescents
Overcome the evil one, They are strong, They know the Word

### Spiritual parents
They know him who is from the beginning
They reproduce (*Implied*)

**God looks for a heart of obedience motivated by grace.** The religious leaders of Jesus' day sought to gain merit with God by reading, studying, memorizing, and quoting the scriptures. Jesus confronts them by saying the scriptures point to him.

## PART 1: BECOMING A DISCIPLE

*You search the Scriptures because you think that in them you have eternal life; and it is they that bear witness about me,* **John 5:39 ESV**

Once we realize the scriptures are about Jesus, by all means read, study, memorize, quote, and most importantly obey. Our obedience is to a person. **The goal of biblical instruction is relationship to Jesus, not simply knowledge.**

*Jesus came and told his disciples, "I have been given all authority in heaven and on earth. Therefore, go and make disciples of all the nations, baptizing them in the name of the Father and the Son and the Holy Spirit.* **Teach these new disciples to obey all the commands I have given you.** *And be sure of this: I am with you always, even to the end of the age."* **Matthew 28:18-20 NLT**

When you said yes to Jesus, your spiritual life began. The Bible provides instructions for the journey, a journey of relationship. Today, let's take a look at the structure of the Bible. Understanding the structure helps us understand how the Bible begins with God's good creation, humanities disobedience, and God's rescue plan through Jesus.

## THE BOOKS OF THE BIBLE
### (66 BOOKS)

| OLD TESTAMENT | 400 Years of Silence | NEW TESTAMENT |
|---|---|---|
| Creation of living things— Return to Jerusalem | | Jesus' birth— Revelation |

| 39 OLD TESTAMENT BOOKS | 27 NEW TESTAMENT BOOKS |
|---|---|
| 5 Books of the Law<br>12 Books of History<br>5 Poetical/Wisdom<br>5 Major Prophets<br>12 Minor Prophets | 4 Gospels<br>1 History<br>22 Letters<br>to individuals and churches |

**Start your Bible reading by asking . . .**

*What did the original writers intend to say; what did they mean? In what context did they write? Historically? Culturally?*

I once heard pastor Charles Simpson quote an old preacher who said, *"The Bible sheds a lot of light on the commentaries."* Charles' point was—the Bible is inspired not what others say about the Bible. Therefore, start with the source. Read and reread the text to see what you can learn from the primary document before you go to secondary study material. A good practice—write down 100 observations of a given passage before you look at what anyone else has to say about a scripture you are studying. Staying with the text long enough for the Holy Spirit to speak to you will prove invaluable over a life-time.

**Here are some clues to effectively studying the Bible**

**1. Text**
    What does the text say?

Is the passage descriptive or prescriptive? Read poetry as poetry. Read history as history. If you read a description of a phenomenon, read through the eyes of the person experiencing the event (In Joshua chapter 10 the Bible says the sun stood still. Joshua describes the events as they appeared to the observers. We use similar language when we say the sun rose and the sun set). Joshua

**describes** what he sees. Other passages, like Matthew 28:19-20 tell us to "make disciples." Matthew **prescribes** how followers of Jesus are expected to obey. When I look at what the text says, I try to write down as many observations as I can find.

## 2. Context

We've all experienced someone taking something we've said out of context. My wife and I have seven kids, and believe me context matters. He said, she said, can get everyone in trouble. When we approach the Bible, context rules.

What is the context of the passage you are reading? By reading 10 verses before and 10 verses after a given section of scripture, you gain a broader understanding of the context.

Rather than pick an isolated chapter here or there or a verse here or there, read the Bible as it was written, in books. Part 2—Making Disciples takes the book of Romans and unpacks it one chapter at a time. We will read Romans straight through as it was written. If you read a given verse or verses within a given book, remember it sits in a broader context. What sentences are immediately before it, what follows? Get in the habit of looking at the context.

An example of failing to read the context would be claiming there is no God based on Psalm 14:1 which says, "There is no God." Without reading the context, one could claim that the Bible teaches that "there is no God." However, if you look at the context, the verse actually says,

*The fool has said in his heart, "There is no God."* **Psalm 14:1 ESV**

Context matters.

## 3. Supporting Texts

When you read your Bible and come across a topic you find interesting, dig deeper. Look to see if there are other places in the Bible where the topic receives attention. Then compare the passages for greater clarity. This keeps us from simply proof texting to support a myopic view. For example, you may want to look up what the Bible says about "giving" or "baptism".

When we read verses in isolation without looking at other verses on the same topic, we may end up with partial understanding. One example would be looking at verses on poverty.

*A little sleep, a little slumber, a little folding of the hands to rest, and poverty will come upon you like a robber, and want like an armed man.* **(Proverbs 24:33-34 ESV)**

This verse highlights poverty resulting from laziness, but the Bible contains many other verses expanding on causes of poverty, including oppression, injustice, violence, greed, and the overall broken state of the world. James 5:1-4 speaks of the rich taking advantage of the poor by fraud.

"Come now, you rich, weep and howl for the miseries that are coming upon you. ² Your riches have rotted and your garments are moth-eaten. ³ Your gold and silver have corroded, and their corrosion will be evidence against you and will eat your flesh like fire. You have laid up treasure in the last days. ⁴ Behold, the wages of the laborers who mowed your fields, which you kept back by fraud, are crying out against you, and the cries of the harvesters have reached the ears of the Lord of hosts." **James 5:1-4 ESV**

**I like to ask two questions when I read the Bible.**

- **What:** What does the passage say?
- **Now What:** Now what is God saying I need to do about it?

## PRAYER

*Father cause me to hunger and thirst for you and your word. I need you.*
*Holy Spirit fill me. In Jesus' name, Amen.*

# JOURNAL TIME

Use your journal to write down:

What did you learn about God today?

What did you learn about yourself?

What is Your Next Step?

Who do you need to share this information with?

## A LITTLE EXTRA

We've been unpacking 1 John 2:12-14, so far in our study. To apply the principles we learned yesterday. Let's broaden our study. Take some time and read 1 John, the entire book consists of five short chapters. Use your journal to jot down:

What stands out to you in the text? What words appear frequently?

What appears to be the context of the author?

Do you know of any supporting texts, other places in the Bible with similar themes?

# WEEK 2—DAY 3
## 10 PERIODS

N OTICE THE 10 PERIODS (The highlighted words below) consists of 5 pairs, i.e. Life—Death (The first pair). The outline gives a quick overview of the entire Bible. Memorize the diagram.

| | | |
|---|---|---|
| God Gave<br>Adam and Eve<br>LIFE |  | The serpent<br>brought<br>DEATH |
| God led<br>Abraham and Sarah<br>FROM Ur | | God led Israel<br>TO the<br>Promised Land |
| Israel remained<br>TOGETHER under<br>Saul, David and Solomon | | Israel is torn<br>APART under<br>Rehoboam |
| Israel is taken into<br>Assyria—<br>Judah is CAPTIVE in<br>Babylon and Persia |  | Judah<br>(The new Israel) is<br>FREE to Jerusalem |

400 Silent Years

| | | |
|---|---|---|
| Jesus' DEATH |  | Resurrection LIFE |

# JOURNAL TIME

Reproduce the 10 Periods (5 Pairs)

What stands out to you in the diagram?

What do you think God is up to?

If you didn't read through 1 John in its entirety yesterday, now would be a good time.

# WEEK 2—DAY 4
# THE MAIN THEME—
# THE KINGDOM

**The Bible has one uniting theme—The Kingdom of God.**

THE KINGDOM REFERS to the rule and reign of God. In Zambia I heard a pastor describe the kingdom as "The Village of God." When we proclaim the kingdom, we declare the ultimate renewal of all things, but the kingdom goes beyond restoration; it introduces a new creation. The Kingdom is the good news of renewal and re-creation. The kingdom often includes signs and wonders—miracles. We see the miraculous side of the kingdom throughout the pages of scripture, in church history, and today. Joan and I have experienced the miraculous on several occasions in our family; here is one example.

Joan discovered she had placenta previa when she was pregnant with our second child, Corrie. We immediately met with the elders of our church and asked them to anoint Joan with oil and pray for her healing, see James 5:14-15. When Joan returned to her OB/GYN, he confirmed her placenta moved, enabling her to vaginally deliver Corrie. We now have seven children, a blessing highly unlikely had Joan not been supernaturally healed. When you confront illness in yourself or others, I encourage you to make your first response prayer for healing.

Our responsibility is to seek the kingdom, proclaim the kingdom, and demonstrate the kingdom; God's responsibility is to expand the kingdom and establish the kingdom.

The kingdom in the Bible is accompanied by salvation, healing and deliverance. We also experience the tension between the already and the not yet of the kingdom—in the "already" we see the miraculous, during the "not yet" times we are reminded the fulness of the kingdom comes when King Jesus returns, but always start by asking.

## Salvation
Salvation is an event and a process. We are saved. We are being saved. We will be saved.

God's presence manifests, and people come to saving faith in Jesus, or people receive healing, deliverance, or a touch from God. The already of the kingdom may show up as we live out the kingdom in large (public) and small (house to house) settings. Expect the already to show up in your church, in your home, or even at restaurants, or on the streets.

Some friends and I stopped by a Dunkin' Donuts in Columbia, South Carolina on our way to Savannah, Georgia. The woman behind the counter greeted us. I'm not sure what she said, but God whispered in my mind, "she is ready to receive me." We placed our order, and I asked what was going on in her life. She opened up and a few minutes later, I prayed with her to receive Jesus. The future kingdom broke into her current reality. The "already" found she was all ready to receive Jesus.

## Healing
When the kingdom is proclaimed in the Bible, signs and wonders follow.

Ian, our fifth child, was born in Savannah, Georgia, Joan and I were church planting; Ian was born with a hole in his heart. Joan, who is a nurse, knew immediately, when the doctor checked Ian's vitals at birth, something was not right—based on the doctor's facial expression. Over the course of the next year, we monitored Ian's heart condition and asked Father to bring healing. For months, there was no change. When we went in for Ian's one year checkup, Dr. Cossio smiled, and he declared, Ian's heart was functioning normally. Joan knew from her medical training closure does occur naturally for some children; this was her initial thought.

We left the doctor's office, Ian in tow, and stopped at a restaurant across from the hospital. Our waitress had a worried expression on her face. I asked if we could pray for her as we prayed for our meal. She then told us to please pray for her one year old granddaughter who was in Atlanta, Georgia undergoing surgery to close a hole in her heart.

**Deliverance**
When the kingdom is declared, people are set free.

My wife, Joan, and two of our sons, John Michael and Ian, experienced the already of the kingdom when Jesus healed them. When John Michael was three years old, he experienced recurring ear infections. He had tubes placed in his ears to resolve the problem. After the tubes fell out, a normal process, the ear infections returned. The doctor met with us and scheduled a second surgery. Joan and I were church planting in Asheboro, North Carolina at the time and had recently switched health insurance providers. We discovered our new provider would not cover the surgery.

We met with our small group in our home and laid hands on John Michael and prayed for his healing. When we returned to the doctor the next week, he looked surprised and stated, "I'm not sure what happened over the past week, but he does not need surgery." On the ride home, John Michael said he wanted to become a follower of Jesus. Up until this point, he told us he was not interested in being a Christian, not exactly what a pastor wants to hear. I asked why he changed his mind. He said, "Jesus healed me, I want to follow him."

**"Already" and "Not Yet"**
The kingdom is both "already" present and "not yet" complete.

**The Already and The Not Yet . . .** We live between the first and second coming of Jesus. Because of this, the full manifestation of God's rule and reign awaits his return. The evil one opposes the message of the kingdom; Satan ultimately loses. The manifestation of the fullness of God's kingdom is "not yet", but it is coming, because he is coming again. So, we pray . . . "Your Kingdom come" Matthew 6:10 . . . "And do not bring us into temptation but deliver us from the evil one. For Yours is the kingdom and the power and the glory forever. Amen." **Matthew 6:13 HCSB**

We proclaim the message: The King of kings is present. The manifestation of the kingdom began with Jesus first coming. It will reach its fulfillment when he comes again. When Jesus returns, his kingdom will manifest in all of its fullness. Until then, we ask for his kingdom to come and we expect the future to break into our current reality and experience.

Practice declaring God's kingdom. Listen for kingdom promptings. In conversations this week, listen for others to share about things going on in their lives. They may share about a problem, a need, or a concern. Take a moment and ask if you may pray for them. If they agree, say a simple prayer asking for God's kingdom to break in.[12]

Write down the experience in your journal.

---

[12] John Wimber used a five step process of prayer. I've modified it here: 1. Listen to the need as stated. 2. Ask clarifying questions (What is the source of the problem). 3. What is an underlying cause. 4. Pray for the stated need, but listen for the Lord to reveal any additional needs. 5. Follow up with the person (if the prayer is for healing ask how they feel after you pray). Expect God to show up.

# READ THE VERSES LISTED IN THE KINGDOM CHART

| 10 PERIODS (5 PAIRS) | KINGDOM |
|---|---|
| Life: Adam & Eve | Gen. 1:14 Signs<br>Gen. 1:27-28<br>Image, Dominion |
| Death: Serpent | Gen. 3:15 Seed<br>Gen. 9:9 Covenant<br>Gen. 9:13 Rainbow . . . sign |
| From Ur: Abraham, Isaac and Jacob | Gen. 14:18 Melchizedek, Heb. 7:2 king of righteousness,<br>Gen. 17:1-14 Covenant of circumcision, kings, 17:15-17 Sign . . . Child,<br>Gen. 35:11 Jacob kings shall come |
| To (The promised land): Moses, Israel, | Ex. 3:1-12 Burning Bush, sign obedience<br>Ex. 7:3 Signs and Wonders |
| Together: David | 2 Sam.7:1-17 Establish your kingdom, Covenant relationship |
| Apart:<br>Elijah and Elisha | Elijah & Elisha men of miracles, Elijah . . . starting in 1 Kings 17, Drought, Widow, Raising son 2 Kings 2 Elisha started his ministry with Signs and Wonders |
| Captive: Daniel | Dan, 2:44 God in heaven will set up a kingdom, 4: 2-3, 17, 25, 32<br>Kingdom and Signs and Wonders, Dan. 5:18, 21-22; 6:25-28, 14, 18; 7:22, 27, |
| Free:<br>Ezra & Nehemiah | Ezra 1:1-4 Jeremiah prophesied of Cyrus coming |
| Coming of King: Jesus | Matt. 3:2; Matt. 4:17 Repent for the kingdom of God is at hand, |
| Going to declare the Kingdom: Paul | Rom. 14:17 Righteousness, peace and joy,<br>Rom. 15:19 Power of signs and wonders<br>Rev. 5:9-10 A kingdom of priests . . . they shall reign |

# FOUR CHARACTERISTICS OF LIFE IN THE KINGDOM INCLUDE . . .

**Life in the Kingdom is Relational—We *BRING* people to the Father**

"Enoch walked with God . . . " **Genesis 5:24 ESV**

"No longer do I call you servants, for the servant does not know what his master is doing; but I have called you friends, for all that I have heard from my Father I have made known to you." **John 15:15 ESV**

**Life in the Kingdom in Fruitful—We *BUILD* people in the Son**

God designed us to live fruitful lives. The first command he gave was "Be fruitful and multiply . . . " Genesis 1:28 ESV

Jesus said, By this my Father is glorified, that you bear much fruit and so prove to be my disciples. John 15:8 ESV

**Life in the Kingdom is Global—We *SEND* people to the World**

"Be fruitful and multiply and fill the earth . . . " Genesis 1:28

"For the earth will be filled with the knowledge of the glory of the LORD as the waters cover the sea." Habakkuk 2:14

**Life in the Kingdom is "Already" & "Not Yet"—Publicly & House to House**

**The chart on the next page shows life in the Kingdom.**

What is your experience with healing? Perhaps you've experienced God's touch many times, or maybe you've never experienced Jesus as healer. Write down your experience, or lack thereof, in your journal.

| 10 Periods | Life in the Kingdom is RELATIONAL |
|---|---|
| Life: Adam & Eve | Gen. 3:8 God walking |
| Death: Serpent | Gen. 5:22 Enoch walked with God, Gen. 6:9 Noah walked with God |
| From Ur: Abraham, Isaac and Jacob | Gen. 17:1, Abram . . . walk before me Gen. 24:40 Isaac . . . I have walked |
| To (The promised land): Israel . . . the Nation, Moses | Deut. 5:33 Walk in all the ways Lev. 26:9 make you fruitful and multiply you |
| Together: David | 1 Kings 2:4 To walk before me, Psalm 56:13 I may walk before God in the light of life |
| Apart: Elijah and Elisha | 1 Kings 22:41 Jehoshaphat walked, Is. 2:5 Let us walk |
| Captive: Daniel | Dan. 9: 10 Repentance . . . Not Walked, Dan. 6:4 He was faithful, Dan. 9:23, 10: 19 Greatly loved |
| Free: Ezra & Nehemiah | Ezra 7:10 Study, do and teach Neh. 5:9 Walk in fear of the Lord |
| Coming of the King Jesus | John 8:12 Not walk in darkness |
| Going to declare the Kingdom: Paul | Rom. 8:4 Walk according to the Spirit |

| LIFE IN THE KINGDOM IS FRUITFUL | LIFE IN THE KINGDOM IS GLOBAL | LIFE IN THE KINGDOM IS "ALREADY" AND "NOT YET" |
|---|---|---|
| **Gen. 1:26-28** Be fruitful and multiply | **Gen. 1:26** All the earth | **Gen. 3:1** Serpent |
| **Gen. 8:17, 9:1, 7** Be fruitful and multiply | **Gen. 3:15** Seed, **Gen. 10:31, 11:9** languages, nations dispersed | **Gen. 3:1** Did God say? **Gen. 3:8-19** Shame, fear, guilt |
| **Gen. 35:11** Jacob . . . be fruitful and multiply | **Gen. 12:1-3** All the families of the earth, **Gen. 18:18** Isaac . . . all the nations | **Gen. 16:1-6** Hagar |
| **Ex. 7:5** The Egyptians will know | **Ex. 12:38** A mixed multitude | **Ex. 7:4** Pharaoh will not listen |
| **2 Sam. 7:12** I will raise up your offspring | **1 Sam. 17:46** That the world may know **1 Kings 8:43, 60** | **1 Sam. 18:12** Saul feared David **2 Sam. 11** |
| **2 Kings 4:17** She bore a son | **1 Kings 17** Gentile widow, **1 Kings 20:13**, you shall know, **2 Kings 5** Naaman- Gentile | **1 Kings 18** Ahab and Jezebel |
| **Jer. 29:7** Seek Welfare of the city, **Dan. 2:48-49** Honor | **Dan. 6:25** All the peoples, nations and languages | **Dan. 6** Lion's Den |
| **Neh. 9:23** Multiplied children **Ezra 7:6, 28; 8:28, 8:18**, The hand of the Lord, **Neh. 1:10** Strong hand | **Neh. 6:15-16** All the nations | **Neh. 2:10** Sanballat and Tobiah |
| **John 15** Bear fruit, bear more fruit, bear much fruit | **Matt. 28:16-20** All nations | **Matt. 4:1-11** The devil tempts Jesus |
| **Gal. 5:22-23** The fruit of the Spirit | **Rom. 1:5** Among all the nations, **Rev. 5:9-10** Every tribe, and language and nation | **2 Cor. 10:4** Strongholds, **Eph. 6:10** Stand against the schemes of the devil |

# JOURNAL TIME

Use your journal to write down:

How do you see God's redemptive plan unfolding?

Which period or pair would you like to know more about?

Pick a period or pair to read and write down at least 10 observations.

# Week 2—Day 5
# Spiritual Parents—
# God's Will

How to Know God's Will

1 John 2:12-14

### Children
Sins forgiven
They know the Father

### Spiritual adolescents
Overcome the evil one
They are strong, *moral character*
They know the Word

### Spiritual parents
They know him who is from the beginning, longevity of relationship with Jesus
They reproduce (*Implied*).

Turn once again to 1 John 2:12-14. This time take your blue pencil and highlight spiritual fathers, parents. Spiritual parents know how to hear from God. Draw the Following Chart in your journal.

| Bible | Circum-stance | Prayer | People | Desires | Action |
|-------|---------------|--------|--------|---------|--------|
| | | | | | |
| **Stop** What verses are standing out to you? | **Look** What is happening around you? | **Listen** What do you sense God is saying to you? | **Others** What are others you know and trust saying to you? | **Heart** What is your heart's desire? What are your thoughts? | **Your Next Step** What is Your Next Step? |

When making a major decision—or to discover God's will in a situation, especially during times of transition, the following chart may be helpful. In each column, jot down information over a period of days, weeks or even months, it normally takes me about three months to see a clear pattern. Look for alignment across the categories, this may indicate God's revealing his will to you.

Read Exodus 3 and 4. Moses followed a similar pattern. When did Moses stop?

What were his circumstances?

What did he hear?

Were others involved? Read chapter 4 before you answer.

Did Moses desire for Israel to be free? Read chapter 1 and 2 to find out.

What action steps did Moses take?

# Journal Time

Reproduce the six steps of the Stop, Look and Listen Model in your journal. Fill in the columns as you are able and discuss the chart with your friend this week in your one-on-one session.

# WEEK 3
# WALKING IN FREEDOM[13]

## Introduction

### WE ARE IN A SPIRITUAL BATTLE

GOD IS GOOD and filled with grace and mercy. He is for you and not against you.

When your heavenly Father created you, he placed within you spiritual curiosity, mental capacity, and physical desires. God fashioned you to enjoy life to the fullest—to live a life of adventure. However, a battle rages. Although God is good and for you, there is an enemy who seeks to steal, kill and destroy you. The enemy presents counterfeit options as though they were real. The enemy distorts reality and tempts you to settle for less than God's best. The enemy whispers lies about your Father and tells you if you don't try (Fill in the blank), you are missing out.

The battle is for your mind. Satan is a created being who rebelled against God, and was demoted by God; he is now God's enemy, and he is also your enemy. He is not equal to God. The good news is: If you are on God's team, you win! Your victory is guaranteed. However, you are not a passive observer in the conflict; you have a vital part to play.

Satan is the father of lies: he whispers, "You will not win." He also may place this thought in your mind today, "What you are doing

---

[13] I am grateful for many who've taught me much about walking in freedom. Derek Prince, Frank and Ida Mae Hammond, and Neil Anderson stand out in my mind; I highly recommend their teaching, example, and published works. I've gleaned much from their efforts, but I've tried to integrate their teaching in my life and make the core of their message and express it in my own words.

71

today will not work." Or, "This is a waste of time, you have so much to do today." The enemy may say you should stop going through the *Kingdom Discipleship* material; he does not want you to be free. Many people fail to recognize the voice of the enemy because it comes in first person singular, "I think I should leave now." Here are several other weapons the enemy may use against you.

# THE ENEMY'S TOOLS INCLUDE:

### 1. Temptation

"No temptation has overtaken you that is not common to man. God is faithful, and he will not let you be tempted beyond your ability, but with the temptation he will also provide the way of escape, that you may be able to endure it." **1 Cor. 10:13 (ESV)**

### 2. Deception

"But I am afraid that as the serpent deceived Eve by his cunning, your thoughts will be led astray from a sincere and pure devotion to Christ." **2 Cor. 11:3 (ESV)**

"You are of your father the devil, and your will is to do your father's desires. He was a murderer from the beginning, and does not stand in the truth, because there is no truth in him. When he lies, he speaks out of his own character, for he is a liar and the father of lies." **John 8:44 (ESV)**

Jesus' desire for you to enjoy life to the fullest; he came to give you abundant life. However, there is a conflict from a counter kingdom. Satan comes like a thief.

"The thief's purpose is to steal and kill and destroy. My purpose is to give life in all its fullness." **John 10:10 (NLT)**

### 3. Discouragement

"For all of them were *trying* to frighten us, thinking, "They

PART 1: BECOMING A DISCIPLE

will become **discouraged** with the work and it will not be done." But now, *O God*, strengthen my hands." **Nehemiah 6:9 (NASB)**

**4. Fear**

"Then the people of the land **discouraged** the people of Judah and frightened them from building." **Ezra 4:4 (NASB)**

**5. Shame**

"What then? Only that in every way, whether in pretense or in truth, Christ is proclaimed; and in this I rejoice. Yes, and I will rejoice, for I know that this will turn out for my deliverance through your prayers and the provision of the Spirit of Jesus Christ, according to my earnest expectation and hope, that I will not be put to shame in anything, but *that* with all boldness, Christ will even now, as always, be exalted in my body, whether by life or by death." **Philippians 1:18-20 (NASB)**

**Our Weapons are powerful**

"For the weapons of our warfare are not of the flesh, but divinely powerful for the destruction of fortresses." **2 Cor. 10:4 (NASB)**

- The written Word of God
- Prayer in the name of Jesus
- Praise and worship of Jesus
- The blood of Jesus
- Resisting in the name of Jesus
- Obedience to Jesus

"His purpose in all of this was that the nations should seek after God and perhaps feel their way toward Him and find him—though he is not far from any one of us." **Acts 17:27 (NLT)**

## Acceptance Before Performance

Before Jesus taught his first lesson, casted out any demons, or performed any miracles, the Father said he was "well-pleased" with Jesus. Acceptance from the Father preceded performance by the son. The same is true for you. God accepts you based on Jesus' work, not on your performance. You do not have to gain the Father's approval by your good behavior. However, when you surrender your life to Jesus Christ, you desire to live a life reflective of God's good work in you; his acceptance of you. Good works follow out of gratitude not as a means of earning merit. Grace is the unmerited favor of God.

"And the Holy Spirit descended upon Him in bodily form like a dove, and a voice came out of heaven, 'You are My beloved Son, in You I am well-pleased.'" **Luke 3:22 (NASB)**

To understand the Father, examine the life of Jesus. If you want to know God the Father, look closely at God the Son, Jesus reflects perfectly the Father's heart.

"Jesus said to him, 'Have I been so long with you, and yet you have not come to know Me, Philip? He who has seen Me has seen the Father; how can you say, 'Show us the Father?'" **John 14:9 (NASB-U)**

## Love Relationship

God desires a love relationship with you through Jesus Christ. The Holy Spirit lives in you to keep the relationship vibrant. There are two verses to keep in mind today. These two verses are keys to unlocking the chains of bondage in your life.

## Confession to God

If we confess our sins, he is faithful and just to forgive us our sins and to cleanse us from all unrighteousness. **1 John 1:9 (ESV)**

74

## Confession to others

"Therefore, confess your sins to one another and pray for one another, that you may be healed. The prayer of a righteous person has great power as it is working." **James 5:16 (ESV)**

God invites us to talk with him about our past, present and future. Our tendency when we sin is to try to hide. However, our Heavenly Father welcomes us to come and confess our sins to him. Take ownership, don't make excuses. Tell him what you did, tell him you are sorry. Ask him to forgive you. Ask Father to reveal why you chose the counterfeit over the real, or why you perverted the good. Ask him to fill you with his Spirit so you can walk in his ways.

The Bible also talks about confessing our sins to others. The context in James 5:16 seems to be peer to peer—"confess your sins to one another." Freedom emerges when we become vulnerable with friends we love and trust; when we willingly expose lies we're believing, sins we're committing, and places we are failing.

On Wednesday mornings, I meet with three fellow journeyers; our meeting provides a safe place where we can be transparent with each other. I find greater freedom in my life when I do not carry my struggles in isolation. God coded our spiritual DNA to function best in community. We all need people we trust and can be transparent with.

Let's journey together and encounter the living and loving God our hearts long to know. God loves you very much. He desires for you to experience his love. Our love for God increases as we experience God. As we grow in our understanding of God's forgiveness our love for him increases.

The Walking in Freedom section will provide the tools you need to experience greater freedom in your life if you are willing to do the difficult work of self-evaluation and processing. Your freedom awaits.

# ILLUSTRATION:

## Welcome Home, Head, Heart, Hands, Your Next Step

 Welcome Home (God welcomes you!)
Head (The battle is for your mind)
Heart (God's heart is a heart of forgiveness)
Hands (Live open handed not closed fisted)
What is Your Next Step?

*Pray this prayer out loud.*

*Heavenly Father,*

*Thank you for loving me so much and sending your Son to die for me. Thank you for setting me free from bondage. I need you deeply. Reveal your love to me. Rebuke Satan! Render his works powerless in my life today. Protect my family and me from the attacks of the enemy. I yield my entire being to Jesus Christ today. I pray these things in Jesus' name. Amen.*

# WEEK 3—DAY 1
## WELCOME HOME

**John 1:12 (ESV)**
"But to all who did receive him, who believed in his name, he gave the right to become children of God,"

WHEN YOU SAID yes to Jesus, God welcomed you into his family. Regardless of your family of origin, he invited you into your new home. In 2003, Joan, John Michael, Corrie, Laurel, Nate, Ian, Charis, Lottie, Jabez (our family dog) and I left Savannah, Georgia and relocated to a new home in my old town, Myrtle Beach, South Carolina. Prior to the move, we served in pastoral ministry for eight and a half years in Savannah. A few weeks before departing, a therapist friend, who attended our church, took me to lunch. During the course of our conversation, he said, "When you get back to Myrtle Beach, you need to have a talk with your Dad." I laughed and said, "My Dad died in 1989, and I don't talk to dead people." My friend smiled kindly, but we both knew what he meant.

Returning home felt different than I thought it would. Many things looked the same, but a lot of life happened between 1987, when Joan and I left the area, and 2003, when we returned. New buildings, restaurants, and roads replaced familiar companies, favorite eateries, and wooded land. When we departed in the 80s, my family referred to me as, "The baby"—since I was the youngest of eight children. When we returned sixteen years later, my family identity shifted; I noticed my siblings introduced me as, "This is Douglas, the one with seven children." After 16 years away, I went from being the youngest of eight to being the father of seven.

After a few weeks of adjusting from the move, our new life flowed with some semblance of order. Our seven kids attended five different schools, and Joan and I worked as a team to pick up, drop off, and get to the soccer fields in time for practice. I frequented The Living Room, a local coffee shop, each afternoon identifying it as my mobile office.

Charlie dropped by The Living Room most days to get his latte. Charlie and I met through my sister and became fast friends, everyone was Charlie's best friend. One day I made the mistake of telling Charlie I needed to visit my Dad's grave, and I asked him to hold me accountable.

Charlie spent several years in and out of rehab for substance abuse. By the time we met, he had been "clean" for several years, but he took accountability very seriously. So, each day, he'd drop by the coffee shop for his hot beverage, and he'd stop by my table and ask if I'd talked with my Dad yet. His persistence annoyed me. There was only one thing I could do; I switched coffee shops. No, actually, I mustered the courage and about three months after moving into our home at the beach, I drove into the country to the cemetery where my father was buried.

The cemetery sits a few feet away from a two lane road; a chain link fence encloses the burial plots—the entire square yard encompasses an area the size of half a basketball court. Old family names engraved in granite mark ground holding bodies awaiting the resurrection. Farm land hugs the left, right, and back perimeter of the fence. A busy two lane road runs a few feet in front of the graveyard. A couple of football fields behind the tombstones to the left sits a beautiful red brick building with a white steeple attached; the sign out front reads, "Good Hope Baptist Church".

Walking through the gate, my great-grandfather's and great-grandmother's graves caught my eyes—then my grandfather's and grandmother's resting place. I paused pondering the dates. After several minutes, I meandered to the back right corner. I stood before my Dad's headstone—1911–1989. Beside Dad's details Mom's date of birth stared back at me—followed by a dash; her date of death came seven years later, in 2010. In front of my parent's names, a

small stone marker lay flat on the ground with "Infant" inscribed—
my parent's first child, a still birth. My dad's mom died when she
was 42. I wondered how Dad processed the loss of his first child, a
little girl, and the premature death of his mom.

Dad was an interesting, intriguing, fascinating, creative,
wonderful man; he was an entrepreneur. He owned tobacco farms,
a country store, a saw mill, a trucking company, pigs, cows, and lots
of chickens. At 51 years of age, and with a seventh grade education,
Dad decided to move to Myrtle Beach and start a new life. "The
Beach", as he called it, was less than 25 miles east of Good Hope,
but the 30 minute drive presented a world far different from the
agricultural life my dad knew and loved.

Dad bought a hotel, then a second, and acquired his real estate
license. My birth came a few months after the relocation; 23 years
separated my oldest sibling, Odell, and me, and I never experienced
the fields of tobacco and tractors he knew so well. My world included
surfboards, shuffleboard, swimming pools, game rooms, tennis, and
basketball courts. My dad and mom faithfully attended church;
mom worked in the nursery and Dad sang in the choir.

Standing in front of my Dad's grave many thoughts flooded my
mind. I began "the talk" the therapist said I needed to have with my
Dad. I laughed some, cried off and on, expressed gratitude, and
vocalized my anger, angst, and unprocessed fears.

On 21 December 1989, I received a phone call—"Dad suffered a
stroke"; I was 27 years old. Joan and I lived in Raleigh, NC with our
two year old son—John Michael, the first male grandchild bearing
the name Dorman; Dad loved holding and talking to John Michael.
Joan, John Michael, and I got into our blue Oldsmobile and rushed
the four hours, it may not have taken us four, to Myrtle Beach. My
siblings and I rotated hospital visits. I stayed the night and held my
dad's hand; he remained unresponsive, except for a slight squeeze
periodically.

In the cemetery, I knelt down and took a handful of green grass
and laid it on top of the grey granite and said, "Dad, you did hurtful
things to our family and me. You were unfaithful to mom. You
abused alcohol. You failed to love us well. I'm angry about your
leaving me too soon. May the deep disappointments I feel be like
this grass; may they wither, fade, and be blown away by the wind."

Then, I reached down and picked up a small piece of green glass sitting in the gravel; it looked like a piece of a Sprite bottle, but reminded me of the drink Teem—Pepsi-Cola used to carry—we sold the beverage in our hotel drink machine when I was growing up. I placed the curved glass beside the green grass and said, "Dad, your duplicity confused me growing up, and confuses me still. You loved God, your family, your church, and yet you lived a double life. Toward the end, the last ten years of your life, you dedicated yourself fully to God; I am thankful. I too feel duplicitous far too often; like Paul, I do the things I don't want, and fail to do the things I should." I see through a glass dimly.

Reaching down a third time, I picked up a rock the size of my fist, and placing the stone on top of the gravestone and said, "But Dad, you also built some solid things into my life. You enabled all eight of your living children to pursue their educational aspirations—as far as they wanted to go. You provided for our family. You taught us to be entrepreneurs. I choose today, to embrace the good, the solid things."

I closed my Dad talk by saying. "Dad, I release you today. You no longer have to parent me, and I no longer need to seek your approval. Today, I bury you." I then laughed and said, "It is about time, you died 14 years ago." When dad died, there was a freak snow storm in Myrtle Beach; we got 16 inches, being in the south—the funeral home did not possess the needed equipment to break through the frozen grown to bury Dad in 1989.

I prayed a prayer of release and Marden Osgood Dorman finally received a proper burial. Engaging in "the talk" enabled me, for the first time since saying yes to Jesus at age nine, to call my Heavenly Father, "Dad". I truly felt my welcome as a child of God. A transfer occurred in the graveyard. A few months later, Joan and I launched Your Next Step as a discipleship ministry; I stepped out of the grave and into a new world of freedom and ministry.

**Genesis 50:20 (NLT)**
"As far as I am concerned, God turned into good what you meant for evil. He brought me to the high position I have today so I could save the lives of many people."

Our families of origin greatly impact how we think about ourselves, God, and others. How we think directly impacts our freedom. If our families of origin used abusive language, gave into negative attitudes, or expressed unhealthy behaviors, Satan uses these patterns to influence how we view ourselves; he often plants thoughts in our minds such as, "I am unworthy, stupid, ugly, no good", "I can't ever do anything right", or "I will never amount to anything." Often "I am", "I can't", or "I'll never" statements, do not originate with us; remember, the enemy uses first person pronouns. The enemy, who masterfully deceives, hijacks our language, so he does not get blamed for thoughts he suggests.

Although the devil cannot read our thoughts, only God is all knowing, he does read our words and actions and knows how to trip us up based on what has worked in the past. We often believe lies about ourselves because of words others said to us. Our family's words either brought life or death.

**Proverbs 18:21 (NASB-U)**
"Death and life are in the power of the tongue, And those who love it will eat its fruit."

## Consequences of sin

The sins of our ancestors can also significantly influence us. We possess the authority and power to purposefully break with the sins of past generations.

"Who keeps lovingkindness for thousands, who forgives iniquity, transgression and sin; yet He will by no means leave the guilty unpunished, visiting the iniquity of fathers on the children and on the grandchildren to the third and fourth generations." **Exodus 34:7 (NASB-U)**

## Children of God. God desires to redirect our inheritance. We are now his kids.

"But as many as received Him, to them He gave the right to become children of God, even to those who believe in His name." **John 1:12 (NASB-U)**

*I encourage you to pray this prayer out loud as a declaration.*

*Father, thank you for welcoming me into your home; I am your child. Father, Son and Spirit . . . I submit to you. I resist the devil; he must flee from me.*

*Renounce . . .*

In the section below, you will go through and speak out loud the following renunciations. Why do we speak these words aloud? Because, Satan can't read your thoughts; he is not omniscient, all knowing, only God knows all. When Jesus faced temptation in Matthew 4, he spoke out loud his renunciation of the evil one's attacks. Follow Jesus' example by saying each of the statements below as an announcement to the evil one of his defeat in your life.

- *I renounce the enemy's attacks on me and my family*
- *I renounce any assignments my ancestors spoke over me*
- *I renounce any spiritual pollution passed on by my family*
- *I renounce ethnic bias*
- *I renounce any satanic covenant made using my name*
- *I renounce any curse the enemy has placed on my life or ministry*
- *I renounce ever signing my name over, or having my name signed over to Satan*
- *I renounce all assignments of the enemy against me*
- *I renounce any animal spirit attached to my family*

*I Cancel and Confess . . .*

In a similar way, make the following declarations.

- *I claim purity through the blood of Jesus*
- *I cancel any demonic working in my life or the life of my family*
- *I am purchased by the blood of Jesus*
- *I belong to Jesus Christ and the evil one cannot touch me*
- *I will walk in your blessing Jesus, and not in Satan's curses*

- *I confess I am now part of God's family; I am his child*
- *I ask you Holy Spirit to open my eyes to any areas I need to specifically renounce . . .*

**Pray this prayer aloud as well.**

***Father in heaven,***

***I am glad my inheritance is in You. I break with the sins of my family. I belong to Jesus Christ and yield to his control, and to him alone, in my life. I will not continue to pass on habits, sins, patterns, sicknesses, attitudes, or lifestyles not bringing honor to you. In Jesus' name, Amen.***

# Journal Time

Use your journal to write down:

What did you learn about God today?

What did you learn about yourself?

What is Your Next Step?

Who do you need to share this information with?

# WEEK 3—DAY 2
# HEAD (THE BATTLE IS FOR YOUR MIND)

**Jesus is The Way, The Truth and The Life**

Satan, family, friends, strangers, enemies, our own minds whisper or shout lies to us. Words spoken to us, or by us, implant themselves in us; they get entrapped in our hearts and minds and take root. Let's do some gardening today by uprooting the lies and proclaiming the truth. Nothing is truer about you than what God says. Truth ultimately is a person. Jesus is the person—he is The Truth.

> Jesus said to him, "I am the way, and the truth, and the life; no one comes to the Father but through Me." **John 14:6 (NASB-U)**

> If indeed you have heard Him and have been taught in Him, just as truth is in Jesus. **Ephes. 4:21 (NASB-U)**

## PERSONAL REFLECTION

Lies we believe about God or ourselves can prove difficult to identify and uproot. Satan is a deceiver, one of his greatest deceptions is disguising lies as truth. What do you believe about God? What do you believe about yourself? When you dig deeper than the surface, you may discover your beliefs about self and God don't square with how the Bible identifies God or you.

Pause a moment and ask the Holy Spirit to unveil your eyes. Invite him to reveal lies you currently hold about God and about yourself. After you've taken time to listen, jot down any lies you believe, or have believed, about God, such as, "He is unloving or unkind." "He is distant." "He is angry with me." "He does not love me."

**In your journal, jot down lies you believe, or have believed, about God.**

Then, write down lies you believe, or have believed, about yourself such as, "I do not have what it takes." "No one loves me." "I can't achieve."

**Jot down lies you believe, or have believed, about yourself, be specific.**

After you complete your lists about God and self, pray the following prayer out loud.

## Prayer

*Father,*

*I confess I have believed the lies that I am*
_____.
*I also confess I have believed the lies that you are*
_____.
*I renounce these lies. I announce—Jesus is the Truth. I ask you to cleanse me from lies in Jesus' name. Amen.*

# JOURNAL TIME

Use your journal to write down when you first started believing lies about God, about yourself.

# WEEK 3—DAY 3
# HEART (GOD'S HEART)

I N INDIA, I taught on forgiveness. One of the pastors attending the training showed me the list of people he needed to forgive; it was several pages long. He said most of the people on the list were other pastoral leaders. His ministry outgrew the work of his peers. As his ministry multiplied, so did his critics. Friends and colleagues became jealous; they attacked his methods, his mentoring, and his message. He even received death threats. When he heard the teaching on forgiveness, the Holy Spirit convicted him to give the list of offenders to him. He chose to surrender his grudge to Jesus; he chose to forgive.

In the Democratic Republic of the Congo, I taught on forgiveness. A young pastor came to me as I was getting in our vehicle to leave. With tears in his eyes, he related to me the story of how he held unforgiveness toward his father. He then blurted out, "How can I forgive my father, he is dead." I immediately felt prompted by the Holy Spirit to stand in as a surrogate father. I said, "Let me stand in as your father." He looked a bit shocked, but said "okay" and began listing offences his father had done to him. When he finished, I asked for his forgiveness as though I were his father. The young man wept as he expressed forgiveness. After several minutes, I prayed over him a prayer of blessing. The relief on his face and in his heart visibly manifested with a smile of joy.

On a church retreat in the United States, I taught on forgiveness. After the teaching, I asked people to pair up, and go through the forgiveness exercise together. One of the pairs included a woman in her 50s and another in her 30s. The retreat met in an old farmhouse. The two women went into the kitchen to pray together. A few moments later the younger woman came to me and indicated a problem. She said her partner sat comatose. We walked to the kitchen and there her friend sat in a chair totally non-responsive. I prayed and asked God if the situation was medical or spiritual; I was unprepared for what happened next.

My mind flooded with the following thoughts. "This home reminds her of the home she grew up in." So, I asked, "Does this home remind you of where you grew up?" She snapped awake, glared at me, and with a growling voice, said, "YES!" She then appeared to go back to sleep. I waited, asking the Lord, "What's next?" Again, I did not expect the next series of thoughts.

What I heard in my spirit was, "She was raped in her home by her three brothers when she was five years old." I thought at this point, "Hmm, maybe I ate too much pizza last night. Or maybe it is my allergy medicine." But, I proceeded, by asking for confirmation. When you think God is revealing something to you about someone else, the best way to verify is to simply ask. So, cautiously, I asked, "May I ask you some very personal questions?" Again, the woman opened her eyes and said calmly, "Yes". I then asked, "Were you raped by your three brothers when you were five years old?" Her face contorted and with a guttural voice she screeched, "Yes, and I will never forgive them."

At this point, we had a clear sense God was leading us. I stated, "You know, God would not reveal something so specific, if you were not able to forgive." Her body relaxed and she then blurted out, "Then, I will forgive them." And she did. A few months later, I taught the freedom material in another city. She came to the second training so she could pray with women who suffered from sexual abuse. She interceded for our ministry as a prayer partner until her death several years later.

The Holy Spirit desires to set people free from hurts, habits, and hang-ups; he often reveals hidden matters of the heart. God's heart is for us to walk in freedom and freedom requires forgiveness. Jesus shows us how to live, love, and forgive. When we look at the life of Jesus we see the Father's heart; we see a heart of forgiveness.

Jesus faced injustice, lies, prejudice, hatred, ridicule, abuse, and death on a tree. When we sieve our experiences through the cross, our perspectives shift. The cross does not remove the wrongs we've gone through, but it does enable us to respond as Jesus did. When we take our hurts to the cross, the Holy Spirit empowers us to forgive as Jesus forgave.

Forgiveness provides us with the ability to move past our hurts. When you became a child or God, the Holy Spirit, the very Spirit of Jesus, came to dwell inside of you. Therefore, you have the power to forgive. Satan lies to you saying, "You cannot forgive them", or "You should not forgive those who hurt you or hurt those you love."

On the cross God revealed our need for forgiveness. Like those who crucified Jesus; we need forgiveness for our sins. Like the Savior who took the pain of others' failures and extended forgiveness, we too can take our pain, because of the cross, and extend forgiveness to those who wronged us.

**God enables us to forgive**

"So also my heavenly Father will do to every one of you, if you do not forgive your brother from your heart." Matthew 18:35

**Failure to forgive hurts only one person, YOU!**

Since Jesus forgave us, we can forgive others. When we refuse to forgive, we remain chained to those who wounded us; we do not enjoy freedom. Pluswe prevent and restrict the grace and love of Jesus from flowing through us to others. We carry a harshness, a damaging tone into other relationships.

**Forgiveness doesn't mean forgetting what happened**

Forgiveness does mean choosing to no longer hold the hurts. Through forgiveness we chose to give the offender to God. We unlock the chains from our wrists and hand them to Jesus Christ. We remove ourselves from the place of judgment, and we let Jesus be the Judge.

## Forgiveness isn't a feeling; it is a choice

You chose to forgive. The feelings may or may not follow. However, forgiveness can be accomplished by an act of your will. Don't wait until you feel like forgiving. Ask God to give you the grace, the desire and the power to do his will, to forgive. Then forgive.

## Forgiveness frees us to be all God intends for us to be

## Jesus modeled forgiveness on the cross; he even forgave those who killed Him.

*"Do not grieve the Holy Spirit of God, by whom you were sealed for the day of redemption. Let all bitterness and wrath and anger and clamor and slander be put away from you, along with all malice. Be kind to one another, tender-hearted, forgiving each other, just as God in Christ also has forgiven you. Therefore, be imitators of God, as beloved children; and walk in love, just as Christ also loved you and gave Himself up for us, an offering and a sacrifice to God as a fragrant aroma."* **Ephesians 4:30-5:2 (NASB)**

Don't say, "I will get even for this wrong." Wait for the LORD to handle the matter. **Proverbs 20:22 (NLT)**

**Pray the following prayer out loud.**

*Father,*

*Thank you for reminding me, " I am forgiven of much." Please bring to my mind those whom I need to forgive as I have been forgiven. I renounce the lie, "I need to get even with those who hurt me." I accept the truth of your justice, and trust you, in your goodness, to do what is right. I pray in Jesus' name. Amen.*

*Father, I ask You to reveal the people I need to forgive.*

**Write down the names God brings to mind on a separate sheet of paper you can burn, shred, or tear up.**

Who do you need to forgive? Perhaps, the categories below will prompt memories.

Family Members

Friends

Enemies

Others

## PRAYER

*Father, I confess that I have held un-forgiveness toward*
_____.
*They hurt me by _____.*
*This made me feel _____.*
*I choose now to forgive _____ for hurting me.*
*I pray this in Jesus' name. Amen.*

Once your list is complete, destroy the list as a tangible reminder you are no longer keeping the list.

93

# JOURNAL TIME

Use your journal to write down what you sense God doing in your heart right now.

# WEEK 3—DAY 4
# HANDS

**(We are called to be open-handed toward those in authority over us)**

WHEN I WAS 11 years old, I served water and butter at a restaurant beside our home; I scooped the butter into balls, like miniature ice-cream servings, and placed them in a small bowl. Paul managed the eatery. One day, Paul entered the dining room with a spoon inside an otherwise empty glass. He said, "Douglas, take this glass into the kitchen." The kitchen sat a few feet away to my right, his left. I grew up as the youngest of eight kids and did not like those older than me telling me what to do. After all, Paul was like family. So, I responded, "Paul, the kitchen is right there!", as I pointed to the kitchen doors. The next day, I got home from school, put on my work clothes and headed to the restaurant. When I walked into the restaurant, the supervisor informed me, "Your services are no longer needed." Note to self, "When you have a conflict with your boss, the boss is always right;" this lesson served me well years later.

Serving on a large church staff proved exhilarating. The first two years flew by and included success followed by success. The senior pastor, who came for a traditional Baptist background, functioned with creativity and openness to the Spirit of God. Then, it happened. During a meeting I led, someone spoke in tongues. Our study on spiritual gifts included teaching time and ministry time, a time to apply the teaching. Excitement filled the air as participants grew in their understanding of and participation in using gifts of the Holy Spirit.

On Monday, the pastor summoned me, "In my office." His tone did not emit a joyful invitation to coffee. I entered and sat down. He started in, his bottom lip quivered a bit as his face reddened. "I know this did not happen; I just need you to tell me 'it did not happen.'" It so happened, a participant from the night before was one of the deacon's daughters. She excitedly reported the events of the previous night to some of her friends, and the news reached the pastor's phone late on Sunday night.

During the weeks leading up to "it happened", the staff discussed and read about spiritual gifts and agreed, sign gifts such as healing, tongues, interpretation of tongues, and miracles still happen today. But, sitting in the pastor's office, I realized there was a difference between theory and practice and "it still happens today" did not apply in the steepled building. We resolved the issue by my agreeing it would not happen again as long as I was on staff.

A few months earlier, I had been called into the office, it felt like I was back in middle school where I spent a lot of time in the office. The issue centered around small groups. I was hired to transition the church from an onsite Sunday School model to an offsite small group model. During my interview a couple of years before, I made it very clear, such a move would create tension on philosophies of ministry and would compete for leaders, but the leadership affirmed they counted the cost and wanted to move to an off campus small group model. To be sure we were not just using the same words but a different dictionary, I said, "If I am hired, I will focus on moving the small groups off campus; I will not oversee Sunday School." All agreed, and I was hired.

As I sat before my boss, he said, "Douglas, you've done a good job with our small group ministry. Now, I want you to give the same attention to our Sunday School." I thought he was joking so I laughed. He did not laugh. Assessing facial expression and body language, it quickly became apparent, he was serious. I voiced my objection, as I did later over the gifts incident previously mentioned, and reminded him of our discussion before I started the job. He looked back sternly and stated, "Let me make it plain, either give attention to Sunday School or get your resume ready."

In both cases, the gifts and the Sunday School, I recalled Paul and the spoon in the glass. I opened my hands and said, "As long as I serve with you on your staff, I will honor your requests. Although I disagree, I submit to your authority. I will give attention to Sunday School." Being right was not the issue. God was after something deeper within me; he was uprooting my rebellious spirit.

After a time of trial, difficulty, and chafing. Our staff met on a dock beside a river. The pastor asked, "If you could do anything you wanted to do, and knew you would not fail, what would you attempt for God?" Each person shared around the circle. When my turn came, I shared about wanting to start a new church. To my surprise, all of the staff agreed, they saw my desire as being from God. The deacons then met and they too affirmed my calling to a new ministry. Perhaps they were just ready to be rid of me. The staff and deacons encouraged me to form a team, train them while still on staff, and then launch. They also agreed to financially support the new work.

What if I closed my fist during my office visits? What if I had pulled out my Bible and defended my position? What if I said, "The kitchen is right there!" What if I had gotten my resume ready? A couple of years later at a lunch meeting with my former boss, a couple of other friends, and a new pastor in town, the new guy innocently asked my former boss, "What do you believe about sign gifts." I suddenly lost my appetite. The senior pastor looked across the table at me, his bottom lip quivering, his eyes moistening, and with a shaky voice said, "Ask Douglas, he and I discussed this some time back and my answer was wrong."

Is your hand open or closed toward those in authority over you? In the Bible, an open hand, extended hand, or God's hand being with someone is a sign of blessing. We are to extend an open hand toward those in positions above us as an act of kindness and humility. We often use the phrase—"to lend a hand"—to indicate helping someone out.

Journal a personal story of submission or rebellion—being open handed toward others—or of being closed fisted—toward those God placed in authority in your life.

The enemy erodes relationships, he does not want us to live in harmony. He distorts submission. He hates authority and engenders rebellion and insubordination. He emphasizes protecting our rights, defending our position. He encourages independent thoughts and actions. Saul yielded to Satan's ploy.

"Samuel said, 'Has the LORD as much delight in burnt offerings and sacrifices as in obeying the voice of the LORD? Behold, to obey is better than sacrifice, and to heed than the fat of rams. For rebellion is as the sin of divination, And insubordination is as iniquity and idolatry. Because you have rejected the word of the LORD, He has also rejected you from being king.'" **1 Samuel 15:22-23 (NASB)**

When Samuel addressed Saul's attitude, rather than repent, Saul defended himself and blamed others. How we respond when we are corrected reveals our heart. Heart response either frees us or binds us. When we respond with open hands to those above us; we exude a welcoming tone; but when we are close fisted, we shut down and become defensive. Our attitude toward those in authority in our lives influences how we relate to others. I've been on many worksites where people are close fisted toward their boss. Their conversation with co-workers radiates vitriol, backstabbing, and disharmony; the attitude often gets transported home as well. God places authority figures in our lives to protect us, sharpen us, and strengthen us.

When we rebel against, reject, or resist correction regarding our understanding, our attitudes, or our actions, we open our lives to Satan's attacks, "For rebellion is as the sin of divination, And insubordination is as iniquity and idolatry."

Receiving correction from those in authority, being open handed, is not based on the personalities of those who speak into our lives. Our tendency is to find fault with the messenger, the timing, the tone, rather than accepting the message humbly. We all want to say, "The kitchen is right there!" However, when we submit to direction, correction, input, insights, and influence, we create a posture to receive from God. We can accept God's best because our hands are open and not closed.

**We are to humble ourselves by keeping an open hand toward those God places over us; they serve as coverings to protect us.**

When we rebel or reject those God calls to lead us, we actually rebel against God, and God takes rebellion personally. Numbers 14 tells a story of the people of Israel rebelling against Moses and Aaron. The close fisted ones think they are simply rejecting fallible human leaders. However, Joshua and Caleb reorient the conversation; they say in effect—those who reject human agency/authority actually rebel against God. Let's look at the story as it unfolds.

All the sons of Israel grumbled against Moses and Aaron; and the whole congregation said to them, "Would that we had died in the land of Egypt! Or would that we had died in this wilderness! **Numbers 14:2 NASB**

**Joshua and Caleb speak up on behalf of Moses and Aaron . . .**

"Only do not rebel against the LORD; and do not fear the people of the land, for they will be our prey. Their protection has been removed from them, and the LORD is with us; do not fear them." **Numbers 14:9 NASB**

Did you catch it? The people grumble against Moses and Aaron, but Joshua and Caleb call them out, and say, "Only do not rebel against the LORD." Perhaps, if we realize human rebellion as divine rebellion, we can rethink our position. God puts us under authority throughout our lives. He even structures authority in the church.

**In the Newer Testament, the writer of Hebrews echoes the importance of spiritual authority.**

"Remember those who led you, who spoke the word of God to you; and considering the result of their conduct, imitate their faith." **Hebrews 13:7 NASB**

"Obey your leaders and submit *to them*, for they keep watch over your souls as those who will give an account. Let them do this with joy and not with grief, for this would be unprofitable for you." **Hebrews 13:17 NASB**

"The authorities are sent by God to help you. But if you are doing something wrong, of course you should be afraid, for you will be punished. The authorities are established by God for that very purpose, to punish those who do wrong." **Romans 13:4 (NLT)**

## PRAYER

*Father,*

*I have not accepted direction or correction well. My attitude and actions reveal my heart. I choose to live life with an open posture—I open my hands to receive from you through others. I ask You to forgive me for being closed fisted. Holy Spirit, please reveal areas where my hands are against and not toward those I am called to submit to. I pray this in Jesus' name. Amen.[14]*

---

[14] Obviously, there are times when others seek to lead us in unhealthy or ungodly ways. When influencers are leading in directions **contrary to God's Word, we are called to obey God and not human authority.**

Here is a list of some of the authorities God inserts into our lives. Take a moment to ask God to speak to you about how you are receiving from him through these authorities.

- God
- Parents
- Spouse
- Children
- Peers
- Spiritual leaders
- Government
- Employers

# PRAYER

*Father,*

*My hand has been closed to those I am called to receive from. Forgive me for not being open handed toward* _____. *I ask you to help me receive from those you place in my life. In Jesus' name. Amen.*

# JOURNAL TIME

Write about how you relate to those in authority over you.

# WEEK 3—DAY 5
# WHAT IS YOUR NEXT STEP?

**God calls us to walk in the Spirit and not in the flesh.**

**Pride and sexual distortion prevent many people from walking in the Spirit. God's desire is for us to walk in humility and purity.**

**Prideful Practices**

> "But He gives a greater grace. Therefore it says, 'GOD IS OPPOSED TO THE PROUD, BUT GIVES GRACE TO THE HUMBLE.'" **James 4:6 (NASB-U)**

Ask . . .

What characterizes a humble person? Write down what comes to mind.

"What characterizes a prideful person?"

## Prideful people tend to think

- They are smarter than others
- They can act independent of others
- Their timing is better than God's
- Their judgment is reliable
- Their abilities are enough
- They need to control the situation, or others
- Their time is their own
- They don't need other people
- They don't need to admit when they are wrong
- Pleasing people matters more than pleasing God
- Others should recognize their contribution
- They are holier than others
- Titles make them important
- Their needs are greater than other's needs
- Their family name (We are better than . . . ) is all important
- Material things show how important they are
- Other ways _____

*Father,*

*Father,*

*I ask You to forgive me for my pride. I choose to humble myself before You and others.*

## Sexual Practices

"If you keep yourself pure, you will be a utensil God can use for his purpose. Your life will be clean, and you will be ready for the Master to use you for every good work." **2 Tim. 2:21 (NLT)**

When I was nine years old, my buddy and I frequently playing in the woods near our homes. One day we discovered a fort. Someone, presumably the fort builder, stored several items there. I do not remember what else made up the hidden stash, but I do remember the pornographic magazines. My friend and I returned to the spot several times. I then expanded my intake of pornography by sneaking peaks anytime I entered a store with elicit magazines. Thankfully, by the time I entered the eighth grade, a mentor began to challenge my behavior. The enemy desires to pervert our sexuality; and he often starts when we are young.

# GOD'S DESIGN . . .

### Oneness In Marriage With One Wife And One Husband

Sex is God's idea AND is intended to be reserved for one wife and one husband. Those who embrace God's ideal can enjoy extreme sexual pleasure. God's desire and design is for you to enjoy sexual relations with your spouse, if you are married, and to give you grace to refrain if you are single. However, when we believe the lie that God is withholding something good from us; or, when we violate God's timing, we destroy our ability to receive the gift of sex God wants to give us.

### River[15]

A river running within its banks possesses beauty and power. A river overflowing its banks destroys life and order. Sex inside the banks of God's boundaries (Marriage) is beautiful and powerful. Sex outside of marriage complicates, entangles, and pollutes all involved.

---

[15] I once heard Kay Authur use this illustration.

## Restoration

Thankfully, God is a God of restoration and new beginnings. You can be forgiven and free of past failures done by you or to you. Sex creates a bond between those who engage in it. In marriage the bond produces intimacy. Outside of marriage the sexual bond produces bondage. We are going to break all past bondages today. Once bondages break you can have a great sex life within the boundaries of biblical marriage—between one woman and one man. Removing bondages also creates room to live in singleness with purity of heart and mind.

"Or do you not know that the unrighteous will not inherit the kingdom of God? Do not be deceived: neither the sexually immoral, nor idolaters, nor adulterers, nor men who practice homosexuality, nor thieves, nor the greedy, nor drunkards, nor revilers, nor swindlers will inherit the kingdom of God. And such were some of you. But you were washed, you were sanctified, you were justified in the name of the Lord Jesus Christ and by the Spirit of our God. 'All things are lawful for me,' but not all things are helpful. 'All things are lawful for me,' but I will not be dominated by anything. 'Food is meant for the stomach and the stomach for food'—and God will destroy both one and the other. The body is not meant for sexual immorality, but for the Lord, and the Lord for the body. And God raised the Lord and will also raise us up by his power. Do you not know that your bodies are members of Christ? Shall I then take the members of Christ and make them members of a prostitute? Never! Or do you not know that he who is joined to a prostitute becomes one body with her? For, as it is written, "The two will become one flesh." But he who is joined to the Lord becomes one spirit with him. Flee from sexual immorality. Every other sin a person commits is outside the body, but the sexually immoral person sins against his own body. Or do you not know that your body is a temple of the Holy Spirit within you, whom you have from God? You are not your own, for you were bought with a price. So glorify God in your body." **1 Cor. 6:9-20 (ESV)**

Sexual pleasure releases chemicals in our brains; the joy of sex exceeds most other life experiences. A bond occurs between sexual partners unlike any other bond in life. God's designs sexual bonding to unite husband and wife as one. Oneness is part of the sexual experience.

However, when sexual activity occurs outside of the marriage unhealthy binding, masking as oneness, results instead of healthy bonding, true biblical oneness. These unhealthy bonds occur regardless of the nature of the sexual experience. Even in abuse a bond results.

When I served as a youth pastor, Joan discipled several young women and I discipled lots of young men. We kept seeing a troubling pattern. We'd meet with high school and college students who clearly loved God, but they kept dating people who hindered their pursuit of God. The cycle of dating—breaking up—getting back together—separating puzzled us. The idea of oneness came to mind. Joan and I began asking our mentees about sexual boundaries in their relationships. We discovered those involved sexually experienced a sexual bond, masking as oneness, making separation difficult. Once we discovered this link, we were able to pray with those we discipled helping them break the soul-ties they shared with their partners. Over the years, we've applied these principles with many women and men who have broken sexual bonds to walk in freedom. We've also discovered authors and leaders who describe the bond using different terms: strongholds, addictions, or attachments. Regardless of the title used the result is the same . . . bondage. God desires to break all sexual bondage.

In order to experience freedom from sexual experiences outside of the marriage relationship, the bonds must be severed. The good news is Jesus still breaks bonds and brings true freedom. Sexual contact outside of marriage, including sexual touching, kissing, oral sex, and intercourse, creates bondage; to be free, you need to name each person with whom you have had, or are having, a sexual bond. Before we deal with the individual cases, pray the following prayer out loud.

*Father,*

*Forgive me for using my body wrongly. My body is a temple of the Holy Spirit. I yield my body to You. I choose to walk in sexual purity from this day forward. I choose Your timing. I renounce the lie that God is withholding fun from me sexually. I accept the boundaries of sex within marriage.*

**Galatians 5:16-26 provides and additional lists of acts of the flesh.**
"But I say, walk by the Spirit, and you will not gratify the desires of the flesh. For the desires of the flesh are against the Spirit, and the desires of the Spirit are against the flesh, for these are opposed to each other, to keep you from doing the things you want to do. But if you are led by the Spirit, you are not under the law. Now the works of the flesh are evident: sexual immorality, impurity, sensuality, idolatry, sorcery, enmity, strife, jealousy, fits of anger, rivalries, dissensions, divisions, envy, drunkenness, orgies, and things like these. I warn you, as I warned you before, that those who do such things will not inherit the kingdom of God. But the fruit of the Spirit is love, joy, peace, patience, kindness, goodness, faithfulness, gentleness, self-control; against such things there is no law. And those who belong to Christ Jesus have crucified the flesh with its passions and desires."
If we live by the Spirit, let us also keep in step with the Spirit. Let us not become conceited, provoking one another, envying one another."

*Father,*

*Reveal other ways I am walking in the flesh and not in the Spirit. Pause . . .*

*I confess that I have participated in _____.*
*I ask You to forgive me. I desire to turn from these works of the flesh. I chose to do so today. Come Holy Spirit and fill me now. I ask this in Jesus' name. Amen.*

Use the JESUS page as a declaration.

# JESUS

Once the person has completed confession of each step, give them JESUS.

**J—Justified 😊 (Just as if I'd never sinned) God welcomes you & smiles upon you.**

> "Confess your sins to each other and pray for each other so that you may be healed. The earnest prayer of a righteous person has great power and wonderful results." **James 5:16 (NLT)**

> "But if we confess our sins to him, he is faithful and just to forgive us and to cleanse us from every wrong." **1 John 1:9 (NLT)**

You are now cleansed from all unrighteousness. You have right standing with God.

**E—Extend** I extend God's forgiveness. God's hand of mercy reaches out to you.

> "If you forgive the sins of any, their sins have been forgiven them." **John 20:23a (NASB-U)**

Do you receive God's forgiveness? Do you forgive yourself?

**S—Sword**

> "The sword of the Spirit, which is the word of God," **Ephesians 4:17 (ESV)**

I take the sword of the Spirit, which is the Word of God, and I sever all connection that your sins have had with people, places, things, and feelings. I do this in the name of Jesus. Amen.

## U—Under

"Submit yourselves therefore to God. Resist the devil, and he will flee from you. Draw near to God, and he will draw near to you. Cleanse your hands, you sinners, and purify your hearts, you double-minded." **James 4:7-8 (ESV)**

Do you come under God's umbrella of authority to walk in His ways? God will now draw near to you.

## S—Shatter

"Is not My word like fire?" declares the LORD, "and like a hammer which shatters a rock? **Jeremiah 23:29 (NASB-U)**

I take God's Word like a hammer and I shatter all that remains of what we cut with the sword. I now shatter any memories associated with these sins (Any thoughts, sounds, smells, tastes, or sensations). I do this in Jesus' name. Amen.

Now take a moment and ask God to show you anything else you need to pray.

# JOURNAL TIME

Write down what has been most meaningful to you about **Kingdom Discipleship—Part 1—Being a Disciple.**

Who can you now take through **Kingdom Discipleship**?

What is Your Next Step?

# ABOUT THE AUTHOR

We live between the inauguration of the kingdom, "the already", and the consummation of the kingdom, "not yet." Kingdom Discipleship seeks to make more and better disciples until Jesus return. Douglas and Joan Dorman formed Your Next Step as a discipleship ministry in 2004 after 17 years as church planters. Turning Disciples into Disciple Makers describes the lives of Douglas and Joan Dorman. Together, they teach, train, mentor, and coach others in discipleship, prayer, and leader development. The Dormans utilize a relational—life on life —approach to discipleship and emphasize the importance of using one's home as base for ministry. They have seven children and a growing number of grandchildren.

Douglas completed his Ph.D. in Intercultural Studies at Biola University and Joan graduated with a BSN is nursing from the University of North Carolina Chapel Hill. Douglas and Joan currently serve as Senior Staff with Global Training Network. For more information, visit: www.gtn.org.

To schedule discipleship training with your group email Doug at: dougd@gtn.org